Love Life: Confessions of a Psychologist

About the Author

Liz Scott has been a psychologist in private practice for over forty years, specializing in work with couples. She is also a writer, having published numerous short stories, a self-help book called *Lies: The Truth about the Self-Deception that Limits Your Life* and a memoir, *This Never Happened*, that was published in 2019. Originally from New York, she now lives and works in Portland, Oregon.

Liz Scott

Love Life: Confessions of a Psychologist

Olympia Publishers
London

www.olympiapublishers.com
OLYMPIA PAPERBACK EDITION

Copyright ©Liz Scott 2024

The right of Liz Scott to be identified as author of
this work has been asserted in accordance with sections 77 and 78 of the
Copyright, Designs and Patents Act 1988.

All Rights Reserved

No reproduction, copy or transmission of this publication
may be made without written permission.
No paragraph of this publication may be reproduced,
copied or transmitted save with the written permission of the publisher, or
in accordance with the provisions
of the Copyright Act 1956 (as amended).

Any person who commits any unauthorised act in relation to
this publication may be liable to criminal
prosecution and civil claims for damage.

A CIP catalogue record for this title is
available from the British Library.

ISBN: 978-1-80439-524-0

This is a work of creative nonfiction. The events are portrayed to the best of the author's memory. While all the stories in this book are true, some names and identifying details have been changed to protect the privacy of the people involved.

First Published in 2024

Olympia Publishers
Tallis House
2 Tallis Street
London
EC4Y 0AB

Printed in Great Britain

Dedication

For W, if only

Acknowledgements

Deep Gratitude: To the fine folks at Olympia Publishing. To the Henry Writers: Steve Arndt, Dian Greenwood, Robert Hill, Gigi Little, Laura Stanfill, and especially Sara Guest and Kathleen Lane. To my clients: Because of my work with you, because of your courage and determination, because of all the ways you inspire. To my exes: We had our choreography, which left me at first blaming you for stepping on my toes. Now, though, I understand all the ways I could have been a better partner. To Will: I wonder. I truly wonder. To the blessed few: Keep on truckin'. You give my battered and sometimes cynical heart some hope. To A and E and M: Forever.

PREFACE

"Those who can do, those who can't teach."

George Bernard Shaw

Here's why you might consider what I have to say about marriage: I have experience. Once I tried to add up the number of couples I've worked with over these four-plus decades as a psychologist in private practice. It's well, well into the multiple hundreds. And even in my work with individual clients, issues in primary relationships are topic number one. So, you can believe me when I say that I am a seasoned, experienced therapist whose specialty in couple's therapy gives me some serious cred. You can believe me when I say that there are patterns, challenges and dynamics that I've seen over and over again, so much so that there seems to be at least a modicum of universality. I've witnessed what tends to help and what makes things worse, what brings people closer together and what drives them farther apart. I have a deep understanding of the ways we all can sabotage our desire to maintain a close, intimate relationship. After all this time, with this many people, I feel comfortable claiming that I am quite wise about this.

And here's why you'd be right to be skeptical and wonder why I, of all people, would be someone you'd turn to for advice or opinion or counsel on the subject of marriage: I have experience. I mean, if someone asked you who you'd want to turn to for wisdom on what it takes to maintain a successful marriage over decades, you might think about your grandparents who've been married for a zillion years and still miraculously seem so happy. Or maybe you think of couples in literature: The Bingleys in *Pride and Prejudice*. Or Dante and Beatrice. Precious little in Hollywood except maybe Nick and Nora Charles. Or Jeff Bridges, who seems to have defied the odds of his compatriots. But speaking of movie stars, I doubt you'd turn to Elizabeth Taylor and her seven marriages for advice. I'm nowhere near seven and can guarantee I won't get there. That said, I have four—count'em—four marriages under my belt, the longest being thirteen years. I've been single for twenty-two years now, after my last and most healthy relationship ended with my husband's death, putting a cap on that experience for me.

My relationship with my marital history is complex, and it depends on the day how I might talk about it. I dearly hope I will someday anchor myself in more settled emotional territory around this subject, but that's still aspirational at this point. Something that's helped me inch my way toward this goal is an interview I heard with Nora Ephron quite a few years ago. I haven't been able to find the transcript, but I remember it well. She was "only" married three times, but I remember being so struck by what appeared to be her comfort and lack of self-consciousness when she loud and proud claimed herself to be an expert on the subject simply because, and only because, her multiple marriages gave her wisdom and insight about the institution. She became my exemplar. What stood out from that interview was how at ease with herself she seemed. There was no sign of embarrassment or shame that I could see. It was her tone—not ironic, not defensive. She seemed sincere and unabashed. Of course, who knows what her internal experience was. We all can present in a way that defies what goes on inside. Even so, I've decided to take her at face value, plant a flag at that guidepost, and keep my hiking boots laced.

So, you may decide I'm a credible source of insight into what makes a marriage work or fail. You may not. I sure get it. I don't get to have a do-over for my three marriages that ended in divorce, but I do have some pretty clear insight into what went wrong and what my former partners and I each could have/should have done differently—not that who I am now would want to still be in any of those relationships, because no! My last husband and I each felt that we'd finally created the healthy, sustaining relationship we'd been struggling toward, but we were still in our early life together when he died. Who knows what time would have told. It's no mystery that even the shiniest of things can tarnish over time.

So, with an equal measure of demurral and confidence, what I offer you in these pages is my insight and my failure, my experience and my scars.

PART ONE

POWER

"A crown is merely a hat that lets the rain in."

Frederick the Great

Did you do this as a kid? Stand on a seesaw, straddling the apex, shifting weight between your feet, trying your best to keep it level. Sometimes it worked and you could just hang out, like an expert tightrope walker, at least for awhile, but certainly not forever. Other times, something—or more like someone—would throw you off, and you'd lose your balance.

That seesaw always comes to mind when I think of the concept of power in a relationship—a dynamic that I believe is ubiquitous. And just like how you have to shift your weight trying to maintain balance on a seesaw, the locus of power in a relationship shifts and changes too. It is not a static thing. It's not static, and it takes basically two different forms: a healthy, natural kind and a not so healthy, verging on and sometimes full-on, dysfunctional kind.

An easy shorthand for these two kinds of power is *power over* and *power to*.

Power Over:

Maybe when you think of power in a relationship, you think of a boss and an underling. Or a parent and a child. Maybe in the context of an intimate relationship, you think of an abusive spouse where one person tries to limit their partner's power through threat, isolation or violence. Or when one person in a couple makes all the money or is more highly educated or more successful, career-wise. It's not uncommon that the person who makes all the money feels entitled to make all the decisions (i.e., assumes the power position). Of course, it's not universally true that the person who makes all the money has most of the power, but at the very least, the ground is extremely fertile for a situation where one person has power *over* the other. And in situations like this, their partner, feeling less powerful, often grows resentful and may flail around, maybe finding passive—or more likely, passive-aggressive—ways to protect their self-esteem, read: feel some power.

The most obvious manifestation of *power over* in a relationship is the stuff that's clear to see a mile away to the naked eye, an imbalance that's pretty obvious. You and I might have a judgment about that. In a perfect world, relationships where one person lords power over another would be rare as rocking horse crap. At the same time, there are so many, many ways of doing a relationship. What would be intolerable for me, might suit you just fine. And I know what "worked" for me when I was twenty-five would be poisonous for me today. And maybe what would work for me today might not be my cup of tea ten years from now.

Much as we might wish it were so, not all relationships are founded on balance and equality. In fact, power imbalance might just be the binding agent that brings two people together in the first place. And while it may not look so pretty from the outside, this kind of *power over* the other actually does serve a purpose. We tend to find what we believe we need, sometimes at a conscious level, mostly not. The obvious truth is that we are where we are at any given time, and we only know what we know when we know it. So, the sixty-five-year-old man and the twenty-something girl/woman that marry do so because it suits them for where they each are on their respective life journeys. We can make all sorts of conclusions (read: judgments) about it: she has daddy issues and makes the willing (usually unconscious) calculus to bask in the reflected light of his status in the outside world instead of having to examine what would make her feel proud and magnificent in her own eyes; he's in denial of his mortality and believes in his unconscious, magical-thinking mind that the youth in his bed and the envy he feels from his cohorts will prevent his decay and annihilation. In this scenario, it's a safe bet that the power tips in favor of the one who's been on the planet for four-plus decades longer. It serves them both, maybe not in the most elegant way but at least as a step in their journeys.

Or there's the relationship between a narcissistic partner and a dependent one where the narcissist enjoys/needs to exert their will and the dependent partner accedes in exchange for the perceived comfort of not having to make decisions or take responsibility for themselves. Maybe not your idea of a perfect partnership, but they are where they are, and they know what they know.

When a relationship is established with this kind of imbalance, it's more than possible to ride along for some amount of time and feel that it's working quite well, thank you very much. *I like being the one to make all the decisions, to get my way all the time.* Or, *It's a relief that I never have to make any decisions or feel responsible when things go wrong.* I can see the appeal. The thing is, though, this kind of dynamic wears thin over time. The one who's in the position of more obvious power might eventually find themselves annoyed with a passive partner who always defers and never expresses a preference—might come to experience this as weak and not grown-up and unsexy. There's that inherent taboo about having sex with our children, right? And the one who always accedes, well, it's not hard to imagine the toll that ends up taking because, really, never stepping into your own needs and wants and preferences is a kind of erasure and abandonment of self.

I think one of the trickier things about maintaining intimate relationships over years and years is that people tend to move along in their personal development at different rates, at different times and in different directions. Or maybe one person moves along and the other doesn't. When one or both begin to change, that's when it might be untenable to maintain the structure that first brought them together. To me, that's the good news and the bad news all wrapped up in one. When a dysfunctional dynamic begins to break down for one or both people, they are presented with a choice: 1) stay stuck in unexamined unhappiness together; 2) one person does the hard work of examining themselves and starting on the road of personal growth while the other one persists in blame—not a good prognosis here; or 3) both people screw up the courage to look at their own individual contributions to the unhealthy dynamic and make it a mission to work on their own damn selves. While it may seem like door #3 is the ideal option, it doesn't guarantee that the couple will stay together. In their personal development, they may come to see that they need something altogether different. Also, change is fucking hard. I truly believe we only change when we *have* to; it's that hard. If things are all groovy and your life is humming right along, you wouldn't be inclined to take an unflinching look at yourself or examine the ways you are falling short or scrutinize your own dysfunctional behavior. Even in relationships that are barely limping along, that are functional though numbing, there may not be enough urgency to feel the imperative to change. The Buddha tells us that everything changes. He just forgot to tell us how hard it is to change ourselves, how much we resist, and how easy it is to firmly anchor ourselves in our certainty about all the ways our partner is fucking up.

    I've been in relationships where I was oblivious to the power imbalance but which could, I'm sure, be seen by any person with eyes. I've learned—or I should say I'm learn*ing*—bit by bit through the lived experience of suffering through the consequences of being in each position of the *power over* dynamic—as well as seeing it in hundreds of couples—and I can tell you, it's not an endless picnic. A relationship where one person has power over another is no recipe for a soul at rest.

Power To:

I've always loved this Martha Graham quote: "There is a vitality, a life force, a quickening that is translated through you into action, and since there is only one of you in all time, this expression is unique, and if you block it, it will never exist through any other medium; and be lost. The world will not have it. It is not your business to determine how good it is, not how it compares with other expression. It is your business to keep it yours clearly and directly, to keep the channel open. You have to keep open and aware directly to the urges that motivate you."

For me, what she's talking about here is the beating heart of personal power which is what I mean by *power to*. Personal power is just that: it's personal. It's not about a division of power between you and anyone else. If it's about any relationship, it's about the relationship we have with ourselves. How do we listen to ourselves? Do we value our own beliefs and opinions? How compassionate and accepting of our own flawed selves are we? This relationship with ourselves is the most central relationship we have, and it's crucial to our well-being as well as to all of our interactions. It's the template we take out into the world.

A healthy, stable relationship with oneself = personal power = *power to*.

"Who has the most power?" This is a question I often ask of a couple I am working with. Sometimes they are quick to answer, no hesitation. And often when the answer is quick like that, it's because they agree that one of them has the most. "Him, he has the most," and "Yeah, true, I do." That's an imbalance of power and almost always of the *power over* variety.(Of course, it's not as straight forward as that—more on some of the intricacies later.) Then there are times when I ask that question, and I get puzzled faces and hmms and shoulder shrugs and looks back and forth between the two of them. I take that as a sign that the power in this relationship might be more of the *power to* type and might be more dynamic. More balanced. But I do not mean balanced as in, you get 50% of the power and I get 50%. Again, when I think of *power to,* I think of personal power. Not about how power might be divided in any kind of relationship, but more about our own sense of agency. When we feel enough personal power, we have a bedrock belief in our own basic okay-ness. We value our intuition and our preferences. We are willing to be open, and we are influenceable, not stubbornly dug in. And when personal power is externalized, it is likely to be more generous, creative and humane than the *power over* variety.

I'm going to list some characteristics here, and I know the tendency is to kind of score yourself or believe that you should either fit all or none of the items in each category in order to see any relevance. Please resist that impulse. You might see yourself in four from column A and six from column B. It matters not. I'd just be open to seeing which, if any, of the descriptions on either of these lists resonates for you and if one list fits more than the other.

When someone feels enough sense of *personal power (power to)*, they are more likely to:
- Respect the wishes, preferences and beliefs of others.
- Be open and willing to be influenced and able to accept feedback.
- Know that they are okay.
- Have compassion for themself.
- Believe that they are rightly entitled to their opinions,

beliefs and preferences.
- Are happy for others' good fortune.
- Accept praise.
- Be willing to engage in difficult conversations and potential conflict.
- Be okay with other people not seeing things their way all the time.

On the other hand, when someone does not have a strong enough sense of *personal power,* they are more likely to:
- Feel reluctant to offer up a preference or opinion.
- Feel uncomfortable speaking up for themself.
- Avoid/dislike attention.
- Deflect or distrust praise.
- Be indecisive.
- Need others' guidance and approval.
- Feel an excessive need to please.
- Envy and compare themself to others.
- Avoid difficult conversations and all conflict.
- Feel like they are regularly taken advantage of and disrespected.
- Think that they do more of the work in the relationship and take more of the responsibility when there are problems.
- Feel alone in their relationship.
- Think that their partner always has the last word.
- Believe that their feelings are not taken into account when decisions are made.
- Feel physically or emotionally intimidated.
- Feel regularly disappointed while their partner is content.
- Feel that their needs are not considered.
- Have their own sexual needs ignored while their partner is only concerned with their needs.

It's tempting to look at this last list and tsk tsk about all the ways your partner is being an asshole. And who knows, your righteousness may be spot on. It's just that you might not even find yourself in a relationship like that to begin with if you felt enough of a sense of personal power. And if you allow yourself to stay in a place where neither you nor your partner recognizes and values your unique you-ness, more would happen in a better way if you turned the klieg light of scrutiny on yourself instead of on your partner. In other words, if you find yourself in a one-down position, it helps to remember that a relationship is like a dance—like a series of coordinated and repeated movements that takes on a life of its own—a co-creation, by which I mean be willing to *look at yourself* and how you are contributing to the dynamic.

I've always believed that we humans have an embedded, innate teleology; like a seed, where its destiny is inherent even before it's planted. Its future is contained in its inception. If you plant a carrot seed in loose, organic soil and well-decomposed compost with a pH of 6.0–6.5, in a place where it will get a minimum of six to eight hours of direct sun, with proper spacing from other seeds, in seventy to ninety days, you will inevitably be rewarded with a beautiful, healthy carrot. The seed's destiny. Its goal of full carrot-ness is achieved. I believe that about us too. That in a perfect world, where every child is born into an enriching environment with enough of what is needed to thrive, with no societal and family obstacles (a girl can dream), that each little seed of a human will fulfill its destiny to be his or her perfectly unique self. I realize the carrot metaphor only works to a point. For us more complicated organisms, there are multiple factors at play. There isn't a finish line where we can spike the ball and do the victory dance. Maybe there'd be a finish line in that perfect world, but in the one we've got, not so much.

And one more way to think about the idea of personal power:

physics. I only got as far as physics 101, but I do remember the concepts of center of gravity and center of mass. In the most overly simplified possible definition, it's about the point at which weight in an object is evenly dispersed, and all sides are in balance. In one sense, it's about the stability of an object. So, if you were building a coffee table and you put the preponderance of the weight in the upper right corner, it probably would be a pretty tippy piece of furniture. Objects are more stable if the bulk of the mass is more central. And when we are out in the world, and especially in our intimate relationships, we are also pretty tippy if our sense of power and agency is not located right smack in our core. When we hand our personal power over to other people, we do not have a stable base to operate from. We are not in balance.

And about the intricacies of relationships, where there is an imbalance of power and a clear *power over* dynamic: it's not as simple as one person has power and the other doesn't. In my opinion, the urge toward the fulfillment of our destiny—that teleology—is so strong that we will find ways to exert personal power when we encounter obstacles, internal and external. We will struggle to find a way, directly or indirectly. Elegantly or clumsily. The clumsy, crude ways are the aggressive assertions of power, but there are also many less obvious ways, things you might not think of as power maneuvers. Things like withholding, stonewalling, or "forgetting" to do what you agreed to do, saying yes when you mean no, and many more. Passive-aggressive and less obvious, yes, but attempts to exert *power over* or claim *personal power* just the same. Like when one partner aggressively demands sex, and the other withholds. Hard to tell who's got more power.

I have to remind myself about this all the time: we are all basically after the same thing. We want to feel okay. We want to feel we are valuable as the unique people we are and that we deserve the space we inhabit. Even people who act like creeps and louts, even victimizers—stick with me here—are struggling in their often inelegant, clumsy, misguided, and dysfunctional way to feel okay. It's like what they say you should do if you encounter a bear: make yourself big, stand on a rock, hold up your arms, shout, and bang pots. What I'm saying is that all that bravado, bluster and intimidation almost always stem from fear—fear that is typically unconscious and unacknowledged. It's a defense and compensation against feeling small and impotent and an attempt to actually deny feelings of powerlessness.

Do I need to say that in no way do I mean this as an excuse or justification for bad behavior? Hope not. And also, this is likely of little relevance to people with severe mental illness or personality disorder. But for most of us, if we are not equipped with the tools we need, if we have had too many obstacles put in our way, we will bumble around, struggling to find a sense of okay-ness. So, these passive-aggressive or aggressive-aggressive ways? It's kind of like using a screwdriver to hammer in a nail: right goal, wrong tool.

"The day the power of love overrules the love of power, the world will know peace."

Mahatma Gandhi

CASE NOTES

Suzi, 35; James, 56;
married 13 yrs; 1 son 12 y/o

PRESENTING ISSUES:

↓ communication ↑ fighting
both feeling distant, lonely.

RELEVANT HISTORY:

Suzi: raised in affluent cmmty
2nd kid, sis + 4yrs good student, lots of friends
until 3rd grade when parents divorced

Divorce ↑ hard on S -> ↓ school work ↑ anxiety +
anorexia thru mid-college; anorexia mostly resolved
b4 met J. Enrolled in MSW after college grad

James: only child, adopted, older parents
Popular, ↑ sports, class prez jr + sr yr

Law school after grad; joined big firm, partner track

Previous marriage > 1 yr

- S + J met online, quickly -> couple, broke up w/ ex's

S almost done w/ MSW when PG quit school

Married b4 son born

Stay-at-home mom tho ambiv, never used degree

J always saying he makes $$$

- ## CLINICAL IMPRESSION:

Both appropriate in speech and manner

J took up most of psych space; spoke the most

somewhat rapid and pressured

Affable; sat forward in chair; confident presentation

- S seemed more anxious, tentative in speech; often looked at J (i.e., checked in w/ him) whenever she spoke

If that twenty-one-year age difference jumped out to you, it did to me too. She married her father, you might understandably think. But sometimes a cigar is only a cigar, so I put a pin in that factoid in order to keep an open mind and then moved on to ask, "How can I help you?" I make sure to hear what each person has to say before we get too deep into things since it is most often the case that their answers will be at least slightly different, and it's very helpful to understand the ways in which they see things independently.

James spoke first and without hesitation. He leaned forward on the sofa, and with an authoritative tone, explained that he was increasingly frustrated that they were not communicating. It never seems accurate to me when a couple complains about "no communicating." I mean, even if they were both mute 24/7/365, wouldn't that be some powerful communication? Or if they couldn't agree on anything, if every talk turned into a fight, or if one person cried every time they had a serious conversation—all of those examples seem like mighty forms of communication. Not direct, sure. Not ideal. But communication nonetheless. So, it might be splitting hairs, but to me it's important to reframe: it's not that they *don't* communicate; it's that they don't communicate directly and effectively.

I asked James to give me some examples of how they were "not communicating," and he talked about how it "drives [him] crazy" when Suzi is so "manipulative." He gave a recent example of what happened when some friends invited them to go on a weekend trip to Seattle. He asked her if she wanted to go, and she said okay; they went, and according to James, she was withdrawn and sullen the whole time. It was clear by his tone and the tension in his face that the Seattle trip made him angry, though the word he used was 'frustrated.' He went on to say that Suzi "always does this," and by that, he meant agreeing to do something and then "acting like a bitch."

Being a therapist requires exquisite attention. There is so much to take in: the words the client is saying, *how* they are saying them, what is *not* being said, their body language and facial clues, how the other person in the room listens or doesn't listen and all their physical clues too. And then comes the decision of what to focus on first and what to file away for later. In this case, while James was talking, Suzi folded her arms tightly over her chest, and with what looked to me like a scowl, turned her head away from James. I asked her to tell me how she felt as she listened to what he said. Her answer: "I didn't have much of a choice. We were going to go anyway; it's not like I could say no."

Power. That's where my mind went, even as we were barely fifteen minutes into our first session. It wasn't just the age difference, though, sure, that can set the stage for a power imbalance. But if someone says, "It's not like I could say no," and we find that this is a pattern in their relationship, it's hard to imagine how the issue of power would *not* be relevant.

I asked Suzi what would've happened had she said no:
"He would have been angry."
I said, "And then what?"
"He would have pouted for days."
"And then what?"
"I would feel guilty."
"And then what?"
"It just wouldn't be worth it."

We dug in and some important things started to emerge. Suzi talked about how James made all the money and how that made her feel "less important," and how she thought it meant that he got to make "most of the decisions." She also talked about his verbal style and said—through tears—that she could never win an argument, so "why bother?" I'm going to risk making a generalization here: many of my clients who are attorneys have well-honed verbal skills, and I doubt I could hold my own in an argument with them on my best day. And it's not like there is anything wrong with that style. But if one person is an ace tennis player and the other excels at chess, and they only play tennis, the chess player will likely end up feeling disempowered and defeated time and time again—defeated and disinclined to engage.

After a few sessions, James brought up the topic of their sexual relationship, complaining that he always was the one to initiate and that Suzi was the one who "controlled" whether it happened or not. This is a great example of something I see so often: people need to feel enough of their own *personal power* in a relationship. Without that, they will likely flail around to find ways that help them feel on more of an equal footing, a process that is often less than conscious. Withholding—in this case withholding and meting out sex—is a mighty tool. It's a way of exerting influence and feeling a sense of personal power. Not a very direct or high-level tool, but powerful nonetheless. A helpful reframing: a dynamic like this can be a step on the way to feeling the kind of personal power that helps relationships thrive. It's that *good goal/wrong tool* thing. When we identify a positive goal, the idea is to explore other, more functional ways of achieving it.

When we start to deconstruct issues of power in a relationship, the person who holds more of the obvious, direct power can feel threatened in an understandable way. Yes, James would have to give up some of his control, and that ain't easy. But when we believe that what we may get in exchange for what we relinquish, the calculus begins to make sense. And it's not just James that would have to shift. Suzi would have to be less fearful, feel more deserving, more able to tolerate his moods, and plant herself firmly in the belief that she is an equal partner, and that ain't easy either.

I worked with this couple for just shy of a year and was impressed by how each one of them approached the hard work of changing what had essentially been lifelong habits. Suzi could see how abandonment feelings she'd lived with since her father left the family were contributing to her reluctance to risk James' criticism. She saw that her baseline anxiety contributed to her feeling fearful, making her less willing to assert herself. But take these steps she did. James—motivated at first, I think, by the notion that he would get more of what he wanted (sex) by giving up some of his control—also began to see that they both would be happier if they each felt a sufficient amount of personal power in the marriage. He recognized that what he called his "cockiness" was a form of intimidation and control, and did not like thinking of himself that way. My hunch is that James—an extroverted, highly verbal man who had his whole life been a kind of prince—would still take up a larger proportion of the psychological space in that marriage and that Suzi—an introvert by nature who dealt with a baseline of anxiety—would sometimes find it quite challenging to assert herself. But, but, but. Therapy is rock-chipping work, there is no such thing as perfect balance, and not a one of us is perfect.

"Uneasy is the Head that Wears the Crown."

William Shakespeare

Just so you know, I will be doing my level best to access whatever amount of self-compassion I can muster as I write this section. It's embarrassing to look back at so many of my choices, especially all those years ago. I'm guessing some of you can relate. So, by way of passing this on to you, I want to help myself by remembering something my beloved, late therapist used to talk about. It's something that has reliably helped me when I'm at a point like this, where I am about to expose some really, truly not-very-pretty stuff about myself. This: the distinction between humility and humiliation. They are close cousins, for sure, and have the same root, the Latin word **humilis**, meaning *low and of the earth*. And the core, initial feeling is the same: that embarrassing, gut-sinking experience of being seen by self and/or others as flawed. These are moments of extreme humanity when we experience the ways we fall short of godliness. We feel *low*. But aside from the common initial experience, the way we *interpret* the feelings of low-ness leads us down entirely different paths. The path of humiliation leaves us feeling shame and disgrace: *I am lower than low, a worm of the earth. I am worthless.* Humility is more akin to embarrassment—no day at the beach either, but it's the low of being *of the earth*, a quality shared by everything that lives. It's that *I'm kind of a mess and so are you* thing.

So, here's my story about power and me in my first marriage. I had my first serious boyfriend when I was fifteen, with silly, meaningless forays starting earlier. In fact, having a boy like me was maybe my highest, most consistent goal until, well—what time is it? It was more important than just about anything. I don't remember one thought about my individual future. I don't think I had one conversation with my mother about what I wanted to do with my life. I don't ever remember a single time when I thought, hmm, maybe I'll be a lawyer or an astronaut or a plumber. Sure, when I was four, I thought I'd be a princess/veterinarian and then when I was eleven, I wanted to be a movie star. That's it. That's where any exploration of future goals stopped. I knew I'd be going to college. Not going was never an option, never even rose to the level of a conscious decision. But the only trajectory that crossed my mind—and even that was only a whisp of a real live thought—was you go to college and then you get married. End of story. I actually find this perplexing, since my mother was absolutely not in the mold of housewife/appendage/stay-at-home-mom/delicate flower. She always worked. She was a serious writer, an artist, and after my parents divorced, a business owner. The modern woman, brave enough to absorb what I'm sure were whispered judgments and pity swirling around among the wealthy wives of the kings of New England in our well-heeled enclave. *Poor dear, that ex of hers just took off and left her in this sad state, having to make her own living, tsk tsk.* When I look back, she was an example by *doing* but against the ground of a complete absence of advice or counsel or guidance. To be fair, I wouldn't have listened to her anyway.

So, I went to a college close to where my boyfriend lived, and I majored in French, and then philosophy and then anthropology and then got a degree in art history—the major that's the butt of most useless college degree jokes. I didn't let classes get in the way of my social life, though. And it's not like I was deliberately looking for a husband, but you go to college and then get married, so who had to be deliberate? That was just the script, and I had my part memorized.

When I left for college, my high school boyfriend and I hadn't broken up. We were hundreds of miles apart but were still together? I guess we were. Maybe? Sort of? It wasn't discussed. So, there I am, a freshman, going to one party after another, missing classes, and only interested in fun. I wasn't two months into my first year when I met R at a frat party. We danced and drank, and I taught him to smoke cigarettes. (R: I'm really sorry. I've always felt so guilty about that and how it led you to a decades-long bitch of a nicotine habit when it was so easy for me to give it up.)I think I must have somehow, someway, also dissuaded him from his daily, and I do mean daily, practice of attending mass—the Catholic kind. If I had to explain this clearly bad influence I had on him, I'd say this: I was provocative, I was wild, I was a novelty in his world, and I presented as confident, verging on cocky, key word being *presented*.

My pattern: I didn't let go of one life preserver until I grabbed another, so there was some overlap between my old boyfriend and this guy who I tagged as in the get-married-right-after-college category. He was smart, fun, a good dancer, someone who said yes to everything, and—I am embarrassed to admit that I believed this at the time and who knows if it was true—someone who liked me more than I liked him, which seemed to be the main criteria for me in a relationship. Plus, he had a good job waiting for him after graduation. Husband material to a silly twenty-one year old with no other plan for her future.

R was a year older than I, graduated and moved to another state to start his good, stable, husband-material job. I don't remember how it actually happened. Was there a proposal? You'd think I'd remember. I do have an engagement ring—somewhere I still have it—I do remember that. And before that, a fraternity pin that I wore proudly as I strutted around campus. See, girls! I snagged one! But—

and here's something that I look back on with embarrassment verging on shame (humility vs. humiliation; humility vs. humiliation!): I don't think he really wanted to get married. But me? Aside from marriage, well, there was no aside for me. So even though I somehow still believed that he liked me more than I liked him, I do think I pushed him, forced him, manipulated him, seduced him—I'm not sure what the right word is, but it's something in that column. Deeply embarrassing, yes. And also, I've come to believe, an example of the power imbalance in that relationship that was there from the get-go.

There were certainly aspects of our early life together that would suggest from the outside that the power tipped in his direction. I followed him to another state where his good, stable job waited for him. He made all the money while I—hmm, what did I do for those two and a half years before my first daughter was born? Not much. But I did control the money that he made, approving or denying even modest expenditures. I decided whether we liked those neighbors or thought they were boring. I was the one who controlled when and if we had sex. I decided when to get pregnant. Whatever you're imagining, you're probably right.

Looking back, I can see that we had a kind of controlling/passive-aggressive dynamic. And this is where the power issue gets more layered and complicated. Anyone with eyes who interacted with us would have concluded that I was the driving force in that relationship, and not in a particularly good way. R was so agreeable and easy-going it would be hard to villainize him, especially when compared to the obviously controlling presence that was me. He was docile Virgo to my bull-headed Aries. I feel on pretty solid ground to say that almost all the outward power was in my pocket, emphasis on the word *outward*.

You can understand, I am sure, how this set-up would wear thin over time. I was the one who finally threw up my hands but—and this is an important *but*—I framed my frustration in a way that blamed him: *I can't stand the way he doesn't assert himself, how he just goes along with everything, how nothing seems to bother him, it's like being in a relationship with a cloud.* Oh, dear girl! How convenient it was to blame him. To focus on him and on the ways you wish he were different. How safe. How misguided.

Dear God of hindsight: You couldn't have helped me out a little? Just maybe a hint or two about exactly how woefully unfinished I was; that would've helped.

PART TWO

LOVE IS BLIND

"Flight from the familiar tedium to new tedium would have for a time the outer look and promise of adventure."

Sinclair Lewis

Sex with a new person can be a blindingly heady experience. If you're heartbroken over a relationship ending, getting involved with someone new can feel like balm to the soul. Your feelings soar. The world is spinning on its axis again. If you are in a stale or dysfunctional marriage, an affair can make you feel alive again and give you a sense of hope that there are other people out there in the world who might be a better partner for you. Make you feel attractive and desired. Wake your body up from a deep sleep. And even if you don't go so far as starting in on an extramarital relationship, meeting someone you spark with, who you fantasize about, and ask yourself, hmm, I wonder what if—even *that* can energize you and make you reconsider your choices; 100% true—all of it.

What I want to focus on now is the *blindingly* part, specifically as it relates to affairs and transitional or rebound relationships. I know there are ethical and moral considerations we could spend hours debating, but salient as those might be, that's not my focus here. Instead, I want to take a look at the more subtle complications that can be out of sight when you're in the throes of this kind of high-octane relationship. It's about the tricky business of being in two relationships at the same time.

Sure, on the face of it, it's a very obvious thing to say—that there might be issues if you are in two relationships at the same time, especially in the case of affairs. That's a big duh! But even if you are positively convinced that you will be leaving your spouse, and that you hate his low-down guts and hope you never have to lay eyes on his lazy ass again, even so, you still are in two relationships at the same time. The "hating his low-down guts" is the giveaway. And more—even if you have signed the divorce papers, rented an apartment, and made multiple trips to Ikea, you are still, to some significant extent, in two relationships. The act of dumping someone or being dumped does not necessarily mean you are free from the relationship, at least emotionally and psychologically. If you are full of anger, if you are jealous about whom your ex is hooking up with, if you are plotting revenge, if your eyes look like you've taken a cheese grater to them, or even some more subtle variations of these scenarios—all of this implies that you are still emotionally and psychologically involved and therefore still in some kind of relationship with the other, even if you never see him or her again and are 100% hoping you never will.

There's a lot of focus on the trust implications of having an affair and also a ton of advice and judgment. I'm not talking about that. What I'm focused on here is a subtle and pesky dynamic that doesn't get much attention: when you are in two relationships at once, each relationship, to some extent or another, is *determined by the other*. In other words, how you see one relationship is inevitably influenced by how you see the other one.

And by influenced, I mean in two ways: 1) through magnification; and 2) through obfuscation.

Here's what I mean. Magnification: Let's say the ink on your divorce papers has not quite dried and you click with someone new. You are fully and consciously committed to *not* comparing your ex with your new partner. That's what you tell your friends who drop the word 'rebound.' You are certain that you see each person for whom he or she is independently. You see qualities in your lover as the qualities you now know you need in your life—and that these qualities have been painfully missing. And those are, of course, important insights to have. Let's say, for example, that you crave warmth and nurturing and that the lack of those qualities was determinative in your decision to divorce. You meet a kindergarten teacher and are bowled over by how warm and loving she is. What happens next has to do with the filters that unconsciously get activated. It's like you put on a pair of glasses that filter out everything except what would go under the column labeled "Nurturing." And under that column, you list any tiny thing that can prove just how nurturing she is—that time she brought you a pastry, how she remembered her second cousin's birthday, the way she smiled at the barista at Starbucks.

At the same time, again mostly unconsciously, the glasses you put on in your spouse's presence will filter out everything *except* what can be construed as the *opposite* of nurturing. This column is labeled "Cold and Withholding," and you'll start compiling evidence—her sharp tone with the children on your trip to Disneyland, how she didn't like that romantic movie you just watched, how she didn't want to go to your work Fourth of July picnic. That pastry swells in mighty proportion, and so does that sharp tone. Each grows disproportionately in your calculus. This filter is most likely not fully conscious, but the result is that certain qualities in one person are underlined and highlighted, as are the opposite qualities in the other person. Okay, fine, maybe the kindergarten teacher, in fact, is the gold medal winner in the nurturing category, and if you identify that this is a quality you crave and have been missing, yay, good to know! But best to be aware of the forces at work.

Another example: Let's say your husband is very passive, a trait that's shredding your very last nerve. And let's say the guy you're having an affair with is only average in his ability to assert himself. Even so, any assertiveness you see in your new guy will make your husband's passivity seem even more pronounced—and your husband's passivity will make your paramour's assertiveness stand out in greater relief. It's like holding a yellow color swatch up right next to a red swatch. As bound and determined as you might be to see these colors independently, each changes the shade of the other.

The thing is, it's only after you are over and done with one relationship that you can adequately assess the next one. How long does that take, you might ask? Damned if I know! Some hints though: if you hear that your ex is in a new relationship and your response is, "Okay, whatever. Hope s/he's happy," you're probably past what would be the rebound stage. If you can't remember the last time you cried about how he did you wrong or that you wrote yet another journal entry about how pathetic she is, you've probably made significant strides in freeing yourself from your ex. You have made this former relationship *small* in your psyche, and that frees up all sorts of space to evaluate any new relationship in a more clear-eyed way without those magnifying glasses on. Just moving out of the house is not enough—or signing a divorce agreement or moving to Montana. A psychological and emotional relationship can continue for a long time. The emotional bonds (and I do not mean only positive bonds) can last far beyond the judge's decree, and these bonds—like that noun implies—keep you in a relationship with your ex.

Obfuscation: Let's say shortly after your divorce you move in with the kindergarten teacher. At first, you will probably bathe in all that warmth and O.D. on chocolate chip cookies, which, btw, sounds amazing. But it's possible that the magnification of these particular qualities also can serve to obscure other qualities that you might not have noticed before, qualities that have been filtered out. Maybe she's passive-aggressive or non-committal or lazy or boring or some other thing that has you screaming into a pillow after some amount of time. Of course, couples invariably need to pass through the developmental dark-side-of-the-moon phase when they start to fully comprehend who the other truly is. After all, it takes years to really know anyone (if ever)—even when we do it one relationship at a time. But if you have been shining a blinding spotlight on her nurturing qualities, you could have obscured from view things that might have given you pause from the get-go. What's even more complicating is that the effects of this dynamic often do not reveal themselves until sometime down the road after big decisions have been made.

I'll end by saying this: been there, done that. More than once. And if I'd read these words at the time, I doubt I would have proceeded any differently than I did. Hardly anyone would. For one thing, when you're in the throes of a new romance, there is so much forward momentum, so much horsepower that we tend to resist information that might suggest that this dreamboat may not actually be so amazing after all. And then there's the whole confirmation bias thing that can make us reluctant to talk to friends or therapists about any doubts we may have when every cell in our body wants this relationship to work. Those chocolate chip cookies are just too delicious to pass up.

It's true that bringing as much of our inner lives to a conscious level tends to lead to better outcomes. In my opinion, that's the ideal path to be on. Sometimes, though, the best to hope for is this: *Yeah, I'm eyes wide open here. But I'm doing it anyway.*

"You can't reason with your heart; it has its own laws, and thumps around things which the intellect scorns."

Mark Twain

CASE NOTES

- Melanie, 38; married to Jeremy 8 yrs, separated 6 mos

PRESENTING ISSUES:
Unhappy in marriage; feeling stuck, divorce?

RELEVANT HISTORY:
- Younger of 2, sis + 3 yrs; grew up in "very white bread" hood.

Parents still married, 43 yrs; "horrible marriage,"
"mo is "boss, domineering."
Fa passive, no waves. Home was 'chilly and distant'.
No affection btwn parents

- Mo doted on kids but "not very motherly." Fa alcoholic?
But never addressed
Average student; spent most of time w/ friends
Met J at party, broke up w/ guy she was seeing

●	*CLINICAL IMPRESSIONS:* *Oriented x 3* *Attractive, well-dressed* *Seemed overly anxious; tripped over words,* *poor eye contact*

There's this thing that often happens in therapy. We can talk for the first session, for the next several and even for weeks before what really brought someone to therapy emerges. Often I can feel it—what's *not* being said. I may not have the slightest clue about *what* it is, just that there are important things that are not being addressed. It's like there's this strong sense of undercurrent in the room. I've wondered about what it is that gives me this sense—maybe some disconnect between *what* the client is saying and *how* they are saying it; maybe something in their body language; maybe something more inexplicable that happens, something on a microscopic, almost mystical level. But however I come by it, when I have this sense, this feeling that my client is avoiding what they really want to talk about, I need to decide how and when to wonder out loud.

Melanie spent the first few sessions with me talking about how she was feeling "suffocated" in her marriage and that she felt "trapped" because she had no viable way to support herself, she was afraid of being alone, and she held a belief that divorce was "shameful." She was the one who initiated the separation from Jeremy, finally feeling that she could not continue to live in what she described as an "oppressive environment." No, she told me, he isn't abusive.

"He's a "really nice guy."
"He's such a nice guy, but he won't give me any space."
"He's such a nice guy, but I feel like I can't breathe."
"He's such a nice guy, but he's so needy."
"He's such a nice guy, but I feel like I'm his mother."

She seemed so nervous to me, shifting in her seat and tripping over her words. She didn't hold eye contact with me for more than a few seconds at a time. You'll probably guess what I say next—*of course* she's nervous! Seeing a therapist is not exactly a clambake at the shore. And this is especially true if it's your first experience, as it was for Melanie. You don't know what to expect, you may not have talked about your concerns with anyone else, and you may have fears about being exposed or even judged. And you're sitting in a small room with a clock, a box of Kleenex, and a complete stranger! Even if you're a therapy pro, meeting with a new therapist can ignite all sorts of feelings and fears.

So, at first I attributed Melanie's nervousness to the understandable feelings about starting this new and vulnerable-making experience and talking about such personal things with someone she'd met about a second ago. But weeks went by, and when most people feel more and more comfortable and safe, for Melanie, not so much. She still stumbled over her words, shook her foot rapidly, and didn't seem to be able to hold eye contact with me.

One of the most important and tricky decisions we therapists have to make is how and when to "confront" the client. (I'm not a fan of that word, "confront." It has such an aggressive feel to me, almost like every direct statement is an aggression. Yeah, if you are up in someone's face, spitting with rage, okay fine, call that a confrontation. But saying something difficult and direct to someone, especially with well-meaning intention? If you think that's a confrontation, it might actually have the effect of making the interaction more fraught. But I just consulted the thesaurus, and I can't find a pithier word, so keep that in mind when you read on.)

Like I said, the two main factors I consider when I want to say something direct and potentially difficult to hear are *when* and *how*. The "how" of it is pretty obvious. It wouldn't be very helpful if I said, "Jeez, Melanie. What the hell's the matter with you? We've been working together for weeks, and you're still nervous? Get a grip, woman!" Not helpful. The "when" part is trickier. As I'm making a decision like this, I consider the quality of my connection with the client—the therapeutic alliance. Have I helped to create a safe space where my client feels respected and heard? Does my client trust me, feel I am genuine and that I have their best interest in mind? I'd never want to broach very difficult or sensitive material if I didn't believe we had established a solid bond.

Then there is the factor of readiness, which can be a tricky calculation to make. I wish I knew exactly what needs to happen to make someone ready to hear and accept challenging feedback. I don't. Sometimes I may get it exactly right. Mostly I either undershoot or overshoot by at least a little. I might send out a trial balloon of mildly challenging feedback and see how my client is willing to take it in and consider. If I get a kind of defensive vibe, pulling back and waiting for a spell might be a smarter decision.

One of the most powerful and beneficial experiences we can have in therapy is using the relationship in the room, in real-time, as a way to wonder about relationships in "real life." It's like we can rewind the tape and do an instant replay. I might say, "I noticed you XXX when I said YYY. Is that something that happens with other relationships in your life?" This kind of in vivo interaction is not often replicated out in the real world, and that makes it a unique feature of a solid therapeutic relationship.

After a few weeks of working with Melanie, I said, "I notice that you seem pretty nervous when we are together. I'm wondering if it's about what's happening here or if this happens for you with other relationships. What can you tell me about that?" Melanie's foot shook even faster; she bit her bottom lip and instantly seemed close to tears. I waited. And waited.

She said, "I'm having an affair."

The undercurrent. There it is. I think we both felt relief at the revelation of this very significant factor, something that had been unnamed but in the room nonetheless since our initial meeting. After all, with this crucial part of the story unacknowledged, our work together would be hampered at the least, and Melanie might very well have been wasting her time and her energy and her money.

This is what happened next. She'd been talking about all the things that "drove her crazy" about her husband, and we'd been going through a pros and cons calculus—of Jeremy and of staying married. And now the calculus shifted. She'd been having an affair with X (she didn't even want to tell me his first name) for about nine months, and though she firmly asserted that she was *not* comparing these two men, it was unavoidable:

"Jeremy just smothers me."

"X is so independent."

"Jeremy seems like a little boy sometimes."

"X is so mature."

"Jeremy can never make a decision."

"X is so assertive."

I wish this story had a happier ending. Melanie and I worked together for about eighteen months, during which time she initiated divorce proceedings and began to make future plans with X, moving in with him before her divorce was final. You'll find a lot of wisdom out there about not jumping from one relationship to another, about rebound and the advice to give yourself sometime after one relationship ends, so you can more easily learn what's important to know before moving on. But lust is some powerful juju and props to you if you can resist. Most of us—read: me—don't. Melanie was all in with X, but after a few months of living together, she began to question her decision. No surprise, really, because, to paraphrase Princess Diana, there were three of them in that relationship, so it was a decidedly crowded.

I had spent some time before she moved in with X talking about this concept: when we are in two relationships at the same time, each one—to some extent—determines the other. Yes, Melanie had left Jeremy physically. Yes, she had seen an attorney and her divorce was underway. Yes, she had moved in with X. The thing is, as much as she protested that she was *not* comparing these two men, her language told a different story. She repeatedly focused on the polarities between the two of them—independent vs. needy; childlike vs. mature; indecisive vs. assertive. It seemed clear to me that even though she was living with X and had initiated divorce proceedings, she was still in an emotional/psychological relationship with Jeremy. He was taking up significant space in her mind and psyche. Being in both relationships at the same time made it hard to have an accurate sense of both these men. For example, the more she experienced X as assertive, the more likely she was to look for evidence of Jeremy's passivity. The more she focused on Jeremy's neediness, the more independent X seemed to her. But these characteristics in each men were exaggerated in her mind by virtue of the fact that, withstanding protest, she was indeed comparing.

Also, because the differences between them had been so figural in her mind, so determinative in her decision to divorce, other factors had been obscured. All the space had been taken up with *he's so this, and he's not at all like that*. It only took a couple of months of living with X before she began to see some troublesome things that had been obscured. Yes, X was independent, a quality she valued. What she didn't love was that he felt no need to inform her of his whereabouts and balked at anything that had the merest whiff of control. And there were other things that had been obscured not only by lust but by the ways he favorably compared to Jeremy. She was bothered that he wanted to spend most of his free time with his friends and did not seem anxious to include her in his socializing. And he was wildly irresponsible. He hadn't filed his taxes for two years, had multiple unpaid bills, and was reckless in ways that frightened her.

    By the time Melanie left therapy, I was heartened that she was willing to examine her own decision-making and the effect of the dynamics from very early in her life which had been at work without her having any conscious awareness. She'd never considered how her parents' marriage had worked as a template for her and that her deeply imbedded model of what it was to be a husband was someone who was passive and unavailable in significant ways. In one of our last meetings, she said, "Looks like I went from one man who had no backbone to one who, well, was nothing but backbone. I went from my father to my mother." That kind of insight is such a huge step in any process of change and growth. At the same time, she again felt stuck. She was living with X and feeling like she'd made her proverbial bed and felt doomed to lie in it. I was so sad to hear what she said during our last meeting: "Maybe I'm just playing out my parents' script—stay even though you're miserable."

    I dearly hope that Melanie will make her way back into therapy at some point. Of course, people terminate therapy for all sorts of reasons: money, time, lifting of mood, fear of continuing, and probably a zillion other things. What's true, though, is that sometimes we need time to integrate what we've learned, let it all sink in and take root. We need more life under our belts before we're ready to dig deeper and peel back the next layer. We need to *live* the new insights. And sad to say, sometimes things just need to get bad enough before we're motivated to dig back in. That's how much we resist change.

"That, my dear, is a horse of a different color."

L. Frank Baum

I entered into my adult life prepared for nothing. Well, not exactly nothing. Because in my junior year I finally had to choose a major, and because Art History is the subject I'd taken more classes in, I *was* prepared to visit an art museum and identify artists without looking at the exhibit labels. Something akin to a party trick. (I can also tie a cherry stem into a knot in my mouth, btw.) But a profession? Not a thought. Which I find quite puzzling. It's about my mother, and I still can't quite square the circle on this one: She was no delicate flower, no prototypical fifties woman. She defied every norm of the time. I think of her as someone consumed by ambition and an insatiable drive to create. Well, more accurately, a drive to be *known* that she chased through one creative venture after another after another. She had fierce ambition and a formidable resume. I call that a norm-breaking model of what it was to be a woman of her time. No way would she have been satisfied with the sole identity of wife and mother. And yet. Given how she was spending her life, it doesn't make a lot of sense that she never once talked to me about what I might want to do with mine. And I'm not even talking about advice. Just some curiosity or a question or two might have helped.

And when I think of how I might have been prepared—or not—for relationships, it's both my parents. What comes to mind first is a hunger that insinuated itself in me when my father left our family, somewhere around my tenth year. It was a hunger that was buried and unrecognized, but firmly ensconced behind the wheel, driving me around every corner. He left and I didn't see him again until I was in my thirties. Doesn't take a 12th level intellect to predict that kind of hunger. As soon as I hit puberty, I became a boy-crazy girl. Not that I was unique among my friends. My best friend had her own version of father issues and parents who divorced, and she was similarly obsessed with boys. In fact, when we were in third grade, we used to decide between us who we would each have as a boyfriend and then inform the boys of our decisions. They, these boys, had no choice. To boot, we had a virtually free-range childhood without supervision or guidance, so our early boy-craziness led us wherever it may, and whatever you're thinking, you're right.

Another thing about my mother: she was definitely a man's woman. You know the type. I think of Lauren Bacall. A woman who uses seductiveness as currency, who is much more comfortable in the presence of men, a woman who has few female friends, if any. My mother had a handful of women friends at any given point, but she always had snippy things to say about them behind their backs. There was a competitive feeling to me, overtones of threat and disdain. I tend to think of this kind of female-to-female bashing as a form of self-hatred. But whatever. The message that came through via osmosis was that the most precious currency was your attractiveness to men.

The upshot is that I was left with a mighty mixed (and unspoken) message: be ambitious but/and your worth lies in your attractiveness to men. At least in my early adult life, the louder message was the one about men.

Okay, so this is how I was launched, with no thought given to my own personal development, no time spent on examining what in the wide world I might actually be interested in, not even a warning that I might have to support myself one day so I'd better be damn sure I could. Nope. To give myself a bit of a break here, this was the prevailing mindset for the largest swath of American women at the time. Even so, all I had was an unexamined, unquestioned assumption that I'd meet my husband in college, and that would be that.

Which I did.

The main upshot of this massive ill-preparedness is that I gave like zero thought about what kind of person would be the best partner for me. I didn't think much about the deeper (!) issues of compatibility or similarity in basic things like values. I met someone who was fun, who was cute, who liked to dance, who liked me and who would marry me right after I graduated from college. I didn't think much beyond the wedding dress and the reception at the country club. No surprise that a setup like that tempts the gods of trouble.

Also, this: shortly after we married, R got transferred to a small—and I mean small—town in Ohio. I'm from New York City. Did I mention that? And went to college in Washington, D.C. This microscopic farm town in the middle of microscopic nowhere, Ohio, felt like living somewhere beyond Andromeda. I had no skill, no profession, no friends, and no idea how to deal with living in this place.

I was a few years late in reading *The Feminine Mystique,* but when I did—stranded and friendless and feeling like a displaced alien—boy, what a smack in the head! That "problem that has no name"? Yup! Friedan landed such a gut punch to women like me in the way she described this unnamed dissatisfaction, this yearning for something more, this isolation and aloneness we felt as we walked through the proscribed female roles we'd been force fed. *Is that all there is?*

It took me a few years and a couple of children to take some action. And maybe a couple of decades for the example of my mother's ambition to mean something to me. We had moved—blessedly—to Cleveland, which felt to me like a first-class ticket to Shangri-La. For one thing, there were several colleges and universities to choose from, and even though I couldn't have told you if I were interested in biology or dance or Italian or accounting, I enrolled in a seminar for women who were returning to work, which, yeah, I know.

That experience turned me into a believer in the awesome power of our inner wisdom, which is so often hidden from our conscious minds. I loved the woman who taught that class, so I asked her what she had studied in college, and she said psychology, so I said okay, psychology, I'll do that too. Not exactly a well-reasoned or even marginally thought-through plan, but it led me to a career that has been so perfect for me, so suited to who I am, and so deeply meaningful that there just had to be some inner wisdom at work. But that's a tangent.

A few years later, when I was studying for my Ph.D., I met someone. I had been feeling discontent in my marriage already, yes. At some level, I absolutely knew it was not the best relationship for me. Of course, none of that was addressed directly between R and me, and the idea of seeing a therapist together never occurred to either of us, even while I was training to be a therapist myself. Yeah, I can't make sense of that either. I was just chugging along in a marginally conscious way, and so was he.

And then.

If I were to diagram this, I would list attributes of R and then those of P, and they would be, almost to a one, the opposite of each other. R was accepting of others to a fault; P had a snarky critique of everyone. R was not highly versed in cultural things like theater, opera, and symphony. P had season tickets. Etc. etc. and so on. The things on P's side of the ledger seemed so vital to me, so central to who I was, so the opposite of the tiny farm town in Ohio. New York City vs. Circleville, Ohio. This must be what I need. This was my answer and my salvation. I will have a career and a partner I jibe with. I'll wear black, put on some Chet Baker and have people over for Perfect Manhattans and repartee. Nick and Nora, that'll be us.

Problem is, the whole red and yellow color swatch thing and how, when you hold them up right next to each other, they affect what you see. I was so busy comparing these two and making a case that I missed some pretty fucking important things that would later prove to be very problematic. Truth be told, I did love those cocktail parties. I did love all that banter. And the trips to New York to gorge on theater. Sure, pretending I gave a shit about wine got old, but I genuinely did love so much of the lifestyle we had. We were so good when other people were around.

Alone together? That was another thing entirely.

Alone together was when all the things that neither of us had noticed or paid attention to or gave much weight to started to reveal themselves. It was like being able to see to the bottom of a stream after the mud that's churned up by some sort of agitation (read: lust) begins to settle. All the stuff that had been obscured by my laser focus on the many ways this relationship was so different from the last relationship bubbled up to the surface. The anger, the withholding, the pettiness, the disappointment, the selfishness—and I mean in both of us—was too clear to ignore.

Alone together, after seven years, became meager and misguided and just plain wrong.

PART THREE

RED FLAGS

"Don't spend time beating on a wall, hoping to transform it into a door."

Coco Chanel

In the 18th century, red flags were used as a warning of flood. In 1836, Mexican general Santa Anna raised a red flag over the tower of San Fernando de Béxar Church to proclaim to the defenders of the Alamo that no quarter would be given. In auto racing, a red flag indicates a stop to the race due to dangerous conditions. And in relationships? Red flags are those warnings, those sometimes-faint murmurs that we should pay attention to, often don't and later wish we had.

We could probably catalog a whole long list of relationship red flags. And what's a deal breaker red flag to one person might be no big deal to someone else. Of course there are things like physical abuse, which we sure hope would be a hair-on-fire red flag to everyone, but sadly, even something so extreme can be rationalized and minimized. But we can talk about some common examples of things to pay special attention to at the beginning stages of any relationship.

I'd divide these concerns into three general categories:

1) Questions about your partner's behavior, personality traits, beliefs, and values (i.e., Do you have similar values and beliefs? Are you uncomfortable with the way your partner treats you and others?)

2) Questions about how you interact with each other (i.e., Are there hurtful or unhealthy relationship dynamics like frequent arguments or avoidance of important issues?)

3) Questions about your own mental and/or physical health (i.e., Are you more anxious, depressed, or isolated? Are you experiencing insomnia or stress-related health problems like high blood pressure, headaches, gastrointestinal issues, etc.?)

And in those general categories, here are more specific examples of things we'd be wise to pay some high-octane attention to:

- Inability to resolve conflicts.
- Controlling behavior or a lack of trust.
- Feeling like you can't fully be yourself.
- Your friends and family members have expressed concerns about your partner or relationship.
- You're typically conceding rather than compromising.
- Difficulty sharing feelings.
- Giving up your friends, interests, or goals.
- Pressure to become too serious too fast.
- Lying or breaches of trust.
- Abuse of any kind (emotional, verbal, physical, sexual, financial, gaslighting).
- Increased symptoms of mental or physical health problems.

I could go on.

Since there is such a long list of possible problem areas, deal breakers, and mismatches, it would seem like navigating our way around them would be easier than it is. Maybe it's that we all need to learn the hard lessons by going through the gauntlet all by our lone-somes. Or that we need to arm ourselves with more insight into why we tend to ignore the red flags, even when they are in plain view. Here are some reasons we might swat away these warnings when they show up in a relationship.

1) Total eclipse of the brain

You're at a party, and your eyes meet across a crowded room, and you feel this force, and you didn't even want to go to this party, but shit, you're in trouble because, like rare earth magnets, you are drawn together. Enter the hypothalamus. It's the part of our brain that stimulates the production of the sex hormones testosterone and estrogen. Now your brain is highjacked. All the pleasure centers of your brain light up like million-watt bulbs. It's amazing. You become obsessed with your new lover; it's hard to concentrate on anything else. And damn if it doesn't feel exactly right to run off to Reno and marry someone you just met a month ago. Nature's little joke, though. Sexual arousal appears to turn off the regions in our brain that regulate critical thinking, self-awareness, and rational behavior, including parts of the prefrontal cortex. You feel so good and connected and loved that it's hard to even see any red flags or notice that your partner has any flaws at all. Sad to say, but lust makes us dumb.

2) Cognitive Dissonance

The theory of cognitive dissonance was developed by Leon Festinger at the beginning of the 1950s after a series of experiments that demonstrated how inconsistencies in our thoughts, opinions and beliefs generate an uncomfortable and motivating feeling; motivating in that we need to do something to decrease the discomfort when our behavior doesn't sync up with our beliefs. One of his studies was of doomsday cult members and their explanations for why the world had not ended as they had anticipated it would. While fringe members of the cult were more inclined to recognize that they had made fools of themselves and chalk it up to live and learn, committed members were more likely to re-interpret the evidence in a way that justified their beliefs.

We all tend to seek consistency, so when there's a disconnect between our beliefs and behaviors, it just doesn't rest well in our bodies. Welcome to the stage the fancy mental gymnastics we use to deal with our discomfort. Like if you are a smoker and also know that smoking causes cancer, you'd likely have to do some brain adjustment to deal with the inconsistency between your beliefs and your behavior. You could discredit the science; quit smoking; or become one of those people who talk about how life is short, so why not? All examples of trying to minimize your cognitive dissonance.

Just like those committed cult members, if we are all-in on a new relationship, if we really, really, *really* want it to work, we are likely to re-interpret, ignore or minimize any negative information. We may ask questions of our partner about their behavior and receive answers, but we often leave the answers alone even if they don't sit well. We want it to work so badly that when something happens that concerns us, we are presented with a choice: deal with it head-on and risk having to walk away or decrease the pressure on our brain by rationalizing, ignoring, or re-interpreting.

Denial can be a mighty powerful force, and by the time we see the warning signs, we're often in so deep that it's hard to get out. So even if we are pretty sure our partner is having an affair, we may not even ask because of what that might mean for us, our families, and our lives. We ignore all sorts of warning signs because we might have to change something—our lives, the place we live, our finances, perhaps even ourselves—if we found out the truth.

3)   We don't trust ourselves

One of the most common reasons we ignore warning signs is our own failure to believe in ourselves. We don't trust our own judgment or our intuition. Perhaps you sense that something is wrong, but proceed anyway. Or, even when you have concrete evidence that your partner or relationship is dysfunctional, you might tell yourself that you're overreacting or focusing only on the negatives. We ignore our gut feelings, signs of disconnection, inappropriate conversations, and foggy details. Our partner convinces us that their explanation is the complete truth and that we are too sensitive, too suspicious, too insecure, and too crazy. Gaslighting. If you haven't seen it, the 1944 film *Gaslight* with Ingrid Bergman and Charles Boyer, stream it tonight and you'll understand.

This is a dangerous game. When we ignore our intuition, it blocks us from knowing primal truths. We learn not to trust ourselves. Whether intentionally or unintentionally—directly or indirectly—when people want their way with us, they will sell us their reality in order to get what they want. We learn to devalue our own concerns and put others' opinions about what we should do and how we should do it above our own. This is definitely one of the biggest reasons for "missing" red flags—that we don't trust our own judgment. When you're haunted by low self-esteem, you doubt even your most basic instincts and feelings. Rather than trusting that gnawing feeling in your gut, you ignore it. When you do this, you're betraying yourself and what you know to be true.

4)   Love is a Long, Hard Road

No one is perfect. You have to compromise. Everyone is different, so of course there will be tensions. We have unrealistic expectations. Yadda, yadda, yadda. True though this all may be, we've been indoctrinated to believe that marriage and committed relationships are hard work. So how do you know which concerns that surface are ones to make a big deal about? Marriage and relationships are indeed hard work, but they shouldn't be so hard that you feel disrespected and at war with your own intuition. When you're in love or want to think the best of someone, you'll make excuses for their harmful behavior. You have to work at it, right? Yes, you have to work at it but...

5) *Anything is Better Than Nothing*

No one can be in an optimal frame of mind to choose a partner when remaining single feels completely unbearable, even terrifying.

6) *The Love of a Good Woman*

This is a dangerous word: potential. You see who he *could* be. If only. All the basic ingredients are there. He will be amazing when he feels more confident, more comfortable, has more success, gets older, feels more secure, takes my advice, goes to therapy, gets a new job, and turns into a different person. It's tempting and ever so ego-gratifying to believe that our love will turn the other into the ideal partner. If I love him hard enough, if I am the best partner to him. If, if and more ifs.

It's easy to get caught up in wishful thinking. You want it to work so badly, or you believe your partner will change, so you disregard the red flags. Your fantasy of what the relationship is or could be prevents you from seeing things as they really are. Love is blind, and hope springs eternal.

7) Confirmation Bias

In the 1960s, cognitive psychologist Peter Wason conducted a number of experiments that demonstrated people's tendency to seek information that confirms their existing beliefs. This is confirmation bias, a cousin to cognitive dissonance. Wason found that we tend to immediately favor information that validates our preconceptions and personal beliefs, regardless of whether they are true or not. Unfortunately, this type of bias can prevent us from looking at situations objectively. Confirmation bias happens when a person gives more weight to evidence that confirms their beliefs and undervalues evidence that could disprove it. It's like wearing glasses with lenses that only let you see the good stuff. You want this relationship to work, so you shine a bright light on all the lovely parts and shove the more problematic ones into a dark corner. The effect is stronger for emotionally charged issues and for deeply entrenched beliefs. We let ourselves forget that there is a dark side to the moon.

8) Vulnerability

You're heartbroken. You've been dumped. All your friends are married. You're lonely. So many things that happen in life can make us feel raw and vulnerable. There's nothing like a new relationship to make us feel hopeful and give us a sense of possibility. It can feel like a source of healing, a bandage on that wound. All the yummy stuff at the start of a relationship is so consuming and compelling and so distracting that there's hardly any room for your pain. Not that your feelings aren't real. But when we are in a state of stress, well, we are just not at the top of our game.

9)   *We don't like to admit we were wrong*

It's hard to admit we've been wrong. No one likes it. And admitting that our relationship didn't work out, or that we misjudged someone, or that we made excuses for bad behavior is an ego challenge for most of us. Pride and fear of failure can keep you in a relationship even when it has devolved into dysfunction. You might be deeply unsettled, but there you are in that beautiful princess dress with 200 people waiting, a six-layer cake and a Led Zeppelin cover band.

When our partners aren't right for us, they have a funny way of showing that truth sooner or later. Taking healthy action takes a dose of radical honesty and some real courage to see these warnings for what they are as early as we can. The truth can be a painful thing, and often it's easier to turn away from it than to turn toward it. The problem with this method, however, is that it only compounds the issues we're experiencing and makes it harder for us to find ourselves beneath the layers of lies and rationalizations and unhappiness. To accept a negative truth about your spouse or loved one is to see them and yourself in a different light.

"It's not what you look at that matters; it's what you see."
                                            Henry David Thoreau

CASE NOTES

- Angie, 38, Chaz, 37
- Married 18 yrs, 3 kids under 12

PRESENTING ISSUES:
A found out re: affair C was having for > 1 yr

RELEVANT HISTORY:
- Angie: from SLCity; devout Mormon family; oldest of 5
- Parents worked, A like parent to sibs
- Model student; teachers loved her...no acting out, rule-follower
- No dating in HS

- Chaz: wealthy family, on trust fund
- Dropped out of HS in 11th grade
- Spent time w/ wine-making, extreme sports, roadie for bands

- Invested in hi-tech co in another state...travels there 4-6 x/ yr
- Met when A in college and C working in record store
- • C was A's 1st bf, 1st sex
- After dating + 1 yr, C wanted to move to Colo to be near skiing; convinced A to drop out of college and move w/ him

CLINICAL IMPRESSION:
- A tearful thruout session
- • C went between comforting and annoyed
- C sometimes inappropriate affect i.e., chuckling when A talking re how she found out re affair

I opened my session with Angie and Chaz as I typically do: *What brings you here? How can I help?* Of course, the first answer is relevant, and I usually write it down as close to verbatim as possible. But I have found that as our meetings proceed, that initial answer is often not really the meat of the problem. This is especially true when there has been an affair. I've batted around so many metaphors over the years, and the one that captures situations like this best for me is this: Your house is on fire (the affair) *and* you have termites (the underlying dynamics in the relationship). It's near impossible to deal with the termites until we can at least get the fire under control. More on this to follow.

In first sessions like this, when a couple is in a crisis, and the pain in the room is palpable, I will almost always save the last fifteen minutes or so to ask them to tell me the story of how they met. Was there an initial attraction? Did they both feel it? Who did most of the pursuing? How long was it before they considered themselves in a committed relationship? And what made him/her different from all the other men/women on earth?

I do this for two reasons: first, there is almost always great information in the story of what drew them to each other. The qualities that were so appealing at first have—as all qualities do—a whole flip side that will inevitably emerge at some point and are often challenging. The dark side of that beautiful mooning phase. For example, someone who is easy-going and agreeable might later be seen as passive and ineffectual. Someone who is assertive and sure of themselves later might be experienced as selfish and insensitive. I'd say this happens roughly about 100% of the time.

It's an understandable fiction to believe that we've found the perfect person with whom we click on every dimension and that our only struggles will be about leaving the toothpaste cap off and about whether the toilet paper goes over or under. For one thing, most of us present our best selves when we meet someone and start dating. We don't tend to get so comfortable at first that we show up in our metaphorical sweatpants with no under-eye concealer. Of course, the problem is that our best self is not our *only* self, and unless you want to be setting the alarm for three a.m. every damn day to shave, put on make-up, do your hair, brush your teeth, put on something cute, and do whatever the hell you can about the not so beautiful parts of your personality, all the other parts of you will be revealed sooner or later. It might be a better world if we followed this advice from Alain de Botton. He suggests that instead of trying to project perfection in the beginning of a relationship, we own up to the ways in which you are kind of "crazy" and encourage the other to do the same.

The other reason I save the last part of the first session with a couple to talk about their beginning together is that almost invariably, when they do, the atmosphere in the room changes dramatically. Up to that point, we've typically been talking about some painful and often scary shit, and it is very unlikely that at the end of an initial session they are going to feel much relief. But when they talk about their origin story, a softening happens. Their shoulders drop, and they look at each other. Sometimes they even smile. It's a much better way to send them home after they've opened the door to some very difficult feelings.

Here is how Angie answered when I asked her what made Chaz different from all other men on earth:

"I'd never met anyone like him. He was nothing like any of the people in my family or my school, or anywhere. I felt like he was a different species, kind of. He was so free and so confident. I loved how passionate he was about the things that interested him. And he didn't automatically buy into societal pressures or expectations. He even looked like a rock star, not like the buttoned-up guys I was so used to."

And here is how Chaz answered:

"Look at her. She's adorable. And the sweetest person ever. She never judged me, and she accepted me for who I am. She wasn't going to be all naggy and critical. I felt so loved by her."

Lots of good information there, right?

But yes, the first thing we had to do was try to douse the fire that Chaz started when he made the decision to consciously-but-probably-mostly-unconsciously have an affair in response to dissatisfaction in his marriage.

(A bit of a sidebar here: I could write a whole other book on affairs—why they start, how to heal and rebuild trust, and when the damage is just too great. But that's not this book.)

Angie and Chaz were equally motivated to heal from the acute pain that happens after an affair is revealed. We worked to at least bring the fire down to embers for several weeks, and each of them seemed earnest and brave and motivated to work on what they could do about the dynamics in their relationship that had been problematic for years.

The termites.

Maybe when you read how Angie and Chaz talk about their beginning together, you are developing some hunches about the things each of them might have been wise to pay more attention to from the jump. Me too. So we dug in and started working on the underlying issues that created the ground for an affair to happen, and when we did, we identified some pretty blazing red super-flags that neither of them—especially Angie—had paid much attention to.

Yes, Chaz was confident and passionate and didn't conform to societal expectations. He was upbeat by nature and adventurous. At the same time, he was self-indulgent and almost exclusively concerned about living his life the way he wanted to without much interest in compromise. He had a markedly underdeveloped sense of empathy, and he was most definitely accustomed to having his pillows fluffed.

And Angie was indeed a sweet and gentle soul. Her instinct was to be a caretaker and to put others before herself. She was compliant and trusting. At the same time, it was hard to get a sense of who she was as an individual human. She almost never expressed an opinion or a preference, even about simple things like what to have for dinner. She never got angry. There was a sort of vaporous quality to her.

I worked with this couple for several months with limited success, I'd say. We did manage to quell the incendiary feelings about the affair, and I do believe that Chaz regretted that he "chose" this way to act out his dissatisfaction. And since his remorse seemed sincere, Angie was able to move along significantly on the road to forgiveness. It also helped that Chaz demonstrated enough forbearance to do some of the uncomfortable things that are helpful to get beyond this stage. (Many of the books that deal specifically with infidelity enumerate these "uncomfortable actions" that require forbearance and facilitate healing, especially in the initial phase after an affair is discovered.)

The not-so-good news is this: Angie was open to looking at all the red flags she'd ignored at the start of their relationship and to reframe these qualities as the flip side of things she admired in her husband. She was in the process of actively trying to figure out if she could wholeheartedly accept Chaz in his full humanity. And what I think is the most significant predictor of a positive relationship outcome, she was willing to look at her own part. She saw not only the things she actively ignored at first but also the ways she contributed to the ongoing dissatisfaction. She began to see that her radical acceptance was a form of extreme passivity. She could understand that all her outward focus on what everyone else needed made her seem dull and unexciting and boring.

Chaz, not so much. Yes, he understood the concept of how we tend to ignore troublesome parts of our partners at first, but hard as I tried, he stayed firmly entrenched in the belief that aside from having the affair, there was nothing he was doing that needed to be changed. He conceded in a most begrudging way that he wasn't "perfect," but he remained firmly rooted in the belief that he had an affair because he needed more excitement and energy than he was getting from his wife.

There comes a point in therapy when continuing seems counterproductive. After weeks and weeks of Chaz firmly rejecting any need for him to change and just as firmly talking about what Angie needed to do differently, it felt to me that I was contributing to this narrative simply by having it repeated week after week. I finally told them I didn't think I could help them and gave them some names of therapists I respect should they choose to work with someone else. My final words to them were these: "I do wish the two of you much happiness. I will tell you that it is my belief and my experience that what is most helpful is not when we point out what the other needs to do differently—as much wisdom as you might have about that—but when we look at ourselves and ask, 'What would it be like to be married to me?'"

"Of course I saw the red flags. I thought it was a carnival."

Anonymous

Have you ever had that jolty experience when you meet someone? I'm talking lusty sparks, like you just got hit upside the head and your sense of time and space telescopes, and you're like, whoa, what the hell is this? You didn't used to believe in fate or the bat-shit theory that there is *one* person for you in all of the universe and that you somehow got lucky enough to meet him at Guarino's restaurant in Cleveland, Ohio, and if you'd stopped at the drugstore on the way to run that errand or if you'd said no instead of yes, you might have missed him and since he is *the* one out of the 7.8 billion, well, end of story, or at least forget about your happy ending. But there he is, and there you are, and he is your person.

You know that feeling?

Run!

That's just what I did *not* do and should have. Just another in the long string of wish-I-knew-then-what-I-know-now experiences I've had in my life. I'm sure I'm not the only one who looks back and wonders exactly what *was* I thinking!

I was around forty years old, which now seems like my babyhood, and back then felt like I was on the cusp of that scary place where women start roaming the desert in sack cloth and ashes. Forty. The year of last chances. I'd already done a wild swing from first man to second man, done a kind of way over there to way over here thing. You'd think that several years into my career as a psychologist, I would be more self-aware. You'd think I'd understand my unresolved issues and the lingering effects of a dysfunctional childhood. You'd think I would take time to acknowledge my fear and examine exactly what *was* so scary about being alone.

You'd think.

My dear friend was married to a guy who ran a tech company. He had a friend. A colleague. A guy who lived in Portland—where? Oregon—hmmm. *He'll be here to meet with me, business stuff. He's single.* What I knew about him: he was divorced, had no kids; he was some sort of hotshot entrepreneur. I tell myself I have nothing to lose. He doesn't live here, so okay, fine, no risk; why not? I'll meet him, said I begrudgingly. The stance I was taking was casual and confident. Trying to convince the world—and more to the point myself—that I can take it or leave it, this relationship thing. It was all guise and affectation, but it went very deep. What lay underneath had not yet poked through the thick layer of my unconscious. That stuff was so deep that it took years for me to even begin to confront and disassemble all that was down there under blankets of defense.

I was ever so nonchalant when I agreed to meet this guy, ever so above any hunger.

The jolt. This intense chemical thing. We locked eyes on that first meeting, and shit! I don't blame myself for believing that having an experience like that meant something. Why would we have this intense physical attraction if it didn't mean something, like maybe even a soul mate thing, even if I didn't believe in soul mates? It's not that there weren't Texas-sized red flags flying from the start. But that electric attraction? It had to mean something bigger. If you could turn your back on that, well, you're a bigger man than I am, Gunga Din.

I spent that whole weekend with him, the time he was there to meet with my friend's husband. I talked to him on the phone after he left, everyday; planned a trip to Portland—that foreign land—just two weeks later. It was clear that even by then, so soon, the ship had sailed, the horse was out of the barn, and the train was headed to the station.

My first visit to Portland. He flew me there, first class. Picked me up at the airport in his red Porsche 911 with armloads of flowers. Yes, he was—is, I suppose—a dazzlingly handsome guy. You probably can't feel more judgment about me than I feel about myself when I tell you how blinded I was by all of that. The combination of the look-over-here glitter and glamour, his hard sell pursuit and my own opacity to myself, well, I slept-walked right smack into the middle of a bona fide relationship by the end of that weekend.

I should tell you what I managed to ignore, justify, and rationalize even in those few short days. At the most superficial level, there was Portland. For the record, I love living in Portland now; in fact, I don't think I'd want to live anywhere else. But that was 1988, and Portland then was not what Portland is now. It was like I was drop-kicked into Sweden, all rosy-cheeked tall blondes, so much time spent talking about kayaking and skiing and hiking and a zillion other sports gerunds that made me feel like such a goddam freak. Not a mention of reading, movie-going, theater-watching, art museum-visiting, dinner partying. I'd never seen so many white people in one place. Me, born in New York City—East Village, to be precise—college in Washington, D.C. and twenty years in Cleveland; I had to keep blinking, adjusting my eyes, trying to make sense of the extreme whiteness of this place. That weekend we went to a Blazers basketball game. The disconnect between the black players on the floor and spectators who were all—and I mean *all*—*w*hite, was supremely unsettling. And there he is, sitting right next to me, mostly riveted by the game, glancing over at me, and wow, that black hair and blue—and I mean blue—eyes, you sure don't see that combo very much, and that deep cleft in his chin, yup, he's gorgeous. But he is clearly not seeing what I'm seeing. Even if I understood or cared about basketball, there was no way I could pay attention. Frickin' ancient Rome and the coliseum, that's what I kept thinking.

He—I guess we'd need to call him my boyfriend now—fit right in. He was born and raised there. This was his place. These were his people. And it didn't take long for the many other differences between us to appear in sharp relief. The first thing he wanted to do on that initial visit was take me to the Portland International Raceway. He parked the car where we had a view of the track, opened the windows and waited for the sound of cars circling the track, Mach ridiculously high, roaring engines and the smell of burning tires. He was spellbound. Those screeching tires were sweet music to him, and I tried. I really did try. You truly can get interested in something by just *deciding* to get interested. So I tried. Yes, I really wanted to cover my ears and had to disguise my yawn and bite my tongue because there was so much I could have said. Afterall, I hadn't shed the theme of cynicism that was the defining characteristic of my last relationship. But okay, I say to myself. Okay, Liz. What's the matter with differences? Differences can be energizing, right? I'd be a pretty small person if I couldn't accept that we had different interests. Okay, fine! He loves the smell of burning tires and swoons at the sound of screeching brakes. And then he tells me his second favorite thing is to fling himself down a mountain in the freezing cold on tiny little pieces of fiberglass— what he called skiing. And how he wants to spend the weekend? Watching football till his eyes bleed, though if he'd actually said it that way, well that would have been at least something. But even in those first few days, it was clear: we had no mutual frame of reference—not with music or books or movies or interests or sense of humor or how to spend time or really any damn thing at all. We had no similarity of values or politics or experience or background or, you name it. Not. One. Single. Thing.

With a nod to Dr. Seuss: Oh, the places I went! I'm not even sure I could map the circuitous, labyrinthine places I went with all this confusing and contradictory information. There was that undeniable and irresistible attraction. And on the other hand, everything else.

Cautionary tale, girls: money and good looks are not the requisite and reliable elements for a fulfilling and healthy relationship. (And p.s., they don't even guarantee good sex.)

I remember being out with a bunch of girlfriends after my second divorce. I can see us there, at a small table in the bar at Night Town Restaurant. A flirtatious bunch, we were. And when the young guy waiting on us brings the second round, I ask him, "So, how many times do *you* think it's okay to be married?" It was a joke. We all laughed, even the waiter. I'm just kidding; that was the vibe. But even now I can feel what was way down there in my fearful heart. Please, someone tell me: how many times is it okay to be married before you will forever be a punch line? The waiter said two, two times, and we all said, yeah, two times. After that, you go from normal to suspect.

But I ignored that wise waiter and turned what should have been a weekend fling into a marriage.

You know how you can get a bead on how people really feel by what they *don't* say? My friends who met him said things like, "I hear really great things about Portland," and "You guys must have really clicked," and "Sounds like he's got a very interesting life," and "Wow." There's lots of information there, don't you think? I could feel it at the time. Way, way, *way* down there, I could feel it. A tiny little murmur, a barely perceptible disquiet. A Maginot Line.

True, at that point I would have needed a super-duper amplifying device to hear what I clearly wasn't ready to hear, but it was there and if I'd been ready, if I'd taken the time, if I'd been brave enough, if I'd been further down the road in my personal journey. If... If... If.

Dear old hindsight. At the start of this all, yes, I may have had a skosh of a smidgen of a hint of insight about why I was so fucking willing to uproot my life in what I'm sure must have looked from the outside as, shall we say, spontaneous (read: impulsive).

(Sidebar: A word about me and decision-making. There's this tendency I have where the more consequential the decision, the more quickly I make it. So, should I buy that house? Marry that guy? Boom. Decided. Do I want the wine glasses at West Elm or the ones at Crate and Barrell? I still haven't decided. And that white shirt? I agonize. I like the white shirt at Banana Republic, but the buttons are so big and that one at Nordstrom, that one's pretty good, but the collar is a little weird, and the placard thing on the one at The Gap is just about a quarter of an inch too wide and I'd be willing to splurge for the one at Mario's if the cuffs weren't the way they are.

I can relate to Elizabeth Gilbert who copped to a history of falling in love fast, making romantic decisions quickly and without much attention to risk. Like her, I have a history of falling in love with *potential*, as opposed to the actual flesh and blood person standing in front of me, waiting for him to ascend to those heights, usually impatiently. The love of a good woman, you know?

So, hindsight. Before I met the guy with the black hair and blue—and I mean blue—eyes and cleft in his chin, I was the divorced mother of two, living in Cleveland, Ohio, which—no offense—is not a place I had ever pictured myself and not a place that felt like home to me. But I did have a life there. I had a house. I had a career. I had a circle of friends, though that circle was shrinking—nothing I'd done but still shrinking through natural attrition. I had a life, but if I sat still long enough, I could feel an energy pushing against invisible boundaries. It was like wearing a sweater that's a size or so too small, where you have to keep adjusting your shoulders, and your body can't ever fully relax. Nothing that had risen in my consciousness enough that I could name it, but in my still moments, a growing sense of dis-ease.

From this distance I can time-travel myself back and see what she—my younger self—couldn't really see herself. How stuck and stagnant she was. How she had nowhere near the courage to make a drastic change on her own and that the only way she knew to shake up her life was by giving herself over to the propulsive power of lust. So, move to a place so entirely different from anything she'd known and marry a guy so weirdly unlike anyone she'd ever even encountered. That oughta do it.

I want to be kind to myself. It truly is hard to make an autonomous choice to up-end your life and make dramatic changes with no guarantee, and all on your own. I wish I'd been brave enough and had enough personal agency. I have so much admiration for people who do. I guess I could have stayed. I could have languished. I could have had a perfectly acceptable life, albeit with the dulled energy I'd learned to live with. So, I'll give myself back-handed props for latching on to the irresistible power of lust to catapult myself out of complacency. I really did shake up my life, and from where I sit now, I can see how important it was for me to push out against the edges of my quotidian existence.

More hindsight: throughout my childhood—my whole life, really—my mother used to talk about all the amazing things I *could* be doing. You're so smart/pretty/talented/better than anyone. You could: Have your own TV Show/Or newspaper column/Write a book(!)/Run for office/Be AMAZING/Be BIG/Be

IMPORTANT/Be FAMOUS. I hated that. I really, truly, in-my-bones hated that. I hated how she was trying to sell me on a false sense of myself. And how I wanted to believe that I truly was all that. I hated all the times she dragged me out to play piano, her friends smiling at her, *Look what a great mother you are*, her nodding yes, *See what a great mother I am.* I hated her on the phone with some random person, *My daughter just did this, and she will be going there, and she always this and always that.* All the reflected glory she craved, me the helium she used to inflate herself.

I'll show you, said my unconscious self. I'll shrink myself. I'll eschew ambition. I'll develop ambivalence in the extreme to most any kind of focus on me. A psychic I went to once said, *You have a very complicated relationship with attention.* Ya think!?

The guy with the black hair and blue—and I mean blue—eyes and cleft in his chin was my second alcoholic. That's one too many to chalk up to coincidence. Usually this suggests family history, but that's where I run smack into a brick wall. One of the truly fucked up things about my family is how there was permanent estrangement on both my mother's and father's sides. I met not one single, solitary relative until I was seventy years old, even though, I came to learn, my mother was the youngest of nine and my father the eldest of three. That probably means I have a zillion cousins. I wish I knew more about them. My own seeming attraction to alcoholics and the co-dependent impulses I see in myself sure make me curious about any history of addiction in my extended family. Alcohol-wise, my mother was a lightweight like me; if you don't count my high school and college days, that is. And my father? I was about ten when he left and then saw him twice again when I was in my early thirties, so who knows. My mother never said a word about addiction where he was concerned. After his death, I did come into possession of some letters between him and my mother after they split, some ugly stuff where he copped to a life of sex, drugs and rock n'roll, but that may have been post-divorce deliverance, as opposed to a diagnosis.

Maybe I'm a unicorn in this family of mine. I can't find any ancestral antecedents, but who knows, maybe it's a generation-skipping thing, addiction. As far as co-dependency goes—and I'm on the verge of gagging even writing that word, it's been so over-used, so bastardized, so casually bandied around—I think I only meet one or two of the original identifying signs. Melody Beattie, who first popularized the concept, defined the signs of co-dependence as:

- Difficulty making decisions in a relationship (*NOPE*).
- Difficulty identifying your feelings (*NOPE*).
- Difficulty communicating in a relationship (*NOPE*).
- Valuing the approval of others more than valuing yourself (*KIND OF*).
- Lacking trust in yourself and having poor self-esteem(*NOT REALLY*).
- Having fears of abandonment or an obsessive need for approval (*HMMM, I'll HAVE TO THINK ABOUT THAT*).
- Having an unhealthy dependence on relationships, even at your own cost (*YUP*).
- Having an exaggerated sense of responsibility for the actions of others (*BUSTED*).

Melody Beattie's first book was titled *Co-Dependent No More: How to Stop Controlling Others and Start Caring for Yourself.* It's the part after the colon. Right there is the recrimination, and okay fine, the insight. It took me years to even see how fucking controlling I had been in relationships. Mind you, it's not the kind of controlling where you're telling people what to do or criticizing anyone for choices. No coercion, no threats, no intimidation. No dominating. No suffocating. I was masterful. At least, I believed I was. True, I had an almost irresistible impulse to take responsibility for others' feelings, to manage their emotions, to fix, make excuses for, interpret, second-guess, anticipate, monitor. So much effort, it's like having about seven full time jobs. But here's the thing: I was a professional, trained in the inner workings of the mind and heart. So those times when I was aware of my efforts to control, I did believe I was pulling it off in a highly sophisticated way, nothing the naked eye could see. *I'm just asking a simple question, no agenda here. Look over there!* Sometimes I think I even fooled myself.

Patting myself on the back, I will say that with awareness and effort—sometimes of the biting my tongue variety—what remains are mere vestiges of that impulse. The biggest challenge is with my adult—underline the word adult—children. You understand.

All this to say, I don't see a family history of addiction, and I'm co-dependent LITE at best.

But back to my second alcoholic. I saw it. Before I agreed to marry him, all the signs were there. Don't blame him. This is on me. After all, you can't bring home a cat and then be upset when it's not a dog. My own willingness to ignore or override the many red flags doomed this marriage from the start. All those irreconcilable differences and alcohol to boot! Eventually, the things that I justified, ignored, rationalized and diminished became as obvious as a circus parade. And still. I was committed to "making it work." I kept thinking of that waiter and how he'd answer, "So, how many times do you think it's okay to be divorced?"

Therapy, endless talks, tears. But each argument chipped away at the already measly balance in my emotional bank account. What we had here was a serious case of cognitive dissonance. It was like I was lighting up a cigarette while I read an article about lung cancer. The things that brought me there to begin with—the exoticism (read: the not me-ness), his legit positive qualities (which now are eluding me), the lust (which I obviously forgot has a short half-life), the glitz (yeah, I know!), his laser focus on winning me over (a drug I've always found hard to resist), and my need to shake up my life (accomplished!)—had worn so thin that any fool—that would be me—could see right through them. Interactions like this didn't help: I say, "Do *you* think you have a problem with alcohol?" and he says, "Sometimes," and my head explodes trying to figure out what in the holy hell that means. Drop after drop of water in a glass that was nearing full.

Here's how it finally ended:

Him: "I need to tell you something."

Very long pause

Him: "I had a part in an unplanned pregnancy."

Even longer pause, during which I absolutely knew I was done because I almost started laughing and had to stop myself from saying, "Oh yeah? Which part?"—*ba-dum-bump*—but controlled the impulse and finally just said:

"Okay, well, I'll be going now."

PART FOUR

GREEN LIGHTS

"Would you like your adventure now, or would you like your tea first?"

James Matthew Barrie

Why, why, why? Why in the Sam Hill is it so frickin' hard to stay married? Statistics vary from year to year, but consistently about half of the people who get married stay and about half walk. So what's up? Well, for starters, life is hard. And for sure, marriage is hard. As Tim Dowling writes in *How to Be a Husband*, "Being married is like sharing a basement with a fellow hostage; after five years there are very few off-putting things you won't know about each other. After ten years there are none." And after twenty-five, thirty years? Fifty? You might be ready to put their eyes out. Familiarity breeds contempt—or a felonious act—as the saying goes. And if you have read John Gottman's work, you know that contempt is not only one of his delineated "Four Horsemen of The Apocalypse"—the relationship habits that predict divorce—it is the most predictive. So, familiarity=good and also familiarity=watch out!

Eli Finkel from Northwestern University spent a year looking at all the sociological, psychological, economic and historical data about marriage that he could get his hands on. His conclusion was that marriage is currently both the *most* and the *least* satisfying that the institution has ever been. Partly it's because we expect so much more. We're not just in it as an economic compact any more, at least not the majority of us. "Americans today have elevated their expectations of marriage and can, in fact, achieve an unprecedentedly high level of marital quality," Finkel writes. Yes, true. But only if they invest a lot of effort. And if they don't or can't, their marriage will be more disappointing to them than a humdrum marriage was to prior generations, to some significant degree, precisely because they've been promised so much more.

Also, even though divorce can be devastatingly hard and often does indeed feel like a failure, making that decision has lost a lot of its stigma. And it's so much easier to divorce than it used to be. Since 2010, every state in the nation has allowed people to leave their spouses without accusing them of anything. In most states, there's no requirement to claim domestic violence or adultery or the anachronistic requirement you might recall from forties melodramas: naming a co-respondent. I bet you can even get a divorce on Legal Zoom.

Also, we live a lot longer. I was shocked to learn that the average life expectancy nearly doubled between 1850 and 2015! That's a shit-ton more years to see the same face across the breakfast table. It's a lot more time for any novelty to wear off and for the downside of familiarity to take hold.

And another thing. People change. We change most often on our own individual timelines, not coordinated with our spouses. The timing of our change is likely different, as is the *direction* of our change. Someone you were so in synch with at the start might be someone you now feel you have to introduce yourself to…*Hi, I don't think we've met. I'm your wife.* It's not uncommon for one person to change in a way that makes what was once a satisfying relationship no longer viable. I've been witness to that phenomenon so many times in my practice that I can't count.

Oh, here's yet another thing. If you have figured out the formula for balancing your individual needs and the needs of your partnership, would you please let me know asap? I get asked this question so often. It's perplexing. Gary Chapman (see below) asserts that we ought to be focused not on getting what we want but on what is best for our partner. He goes on to say that this means letting go of our selfish needs so that our partner's needs can be met. Maybe it's a particularly American reaction I have to this—a focus on the almighty INDIVIDUAL. On the one hand, yes, of course. But I have seen more times than I can count how painful and soul-crushing it can be to subsume your own needs to the extent that you may not even recognize that you actually *have* essential needs, desires, and boundaries, which has me thinking about *The Giving Tree.* I bet you read this book to your kids. Me too. I read it to my own children, believing I was helping them develop a sense of generosity and altruism. But as I moved along in my career and witnessed so many people giving away all their branches and their leaves, reducing themselves to stumps in order to provide for the other, well, now I read it differently. *The Giving Tree* is—I was going to say *evil*—damaging in the message it sends. In a perfect world, we would all be living in *The Gift of the Magi* where we each are so perfectly attuned to our partner's needs and so willing to give that no one ends up feeling that they are in self-renunciation for the sake of the other.

It's a puzzle though, and I believe, is another reason it's hard to stay married.

But maybe now you're thinking of your own happy marriage. Or your parents who've been married for sixty-two years and still dance in the kitchen. Or your best friend in a blissful second marriage. Or Nick and Nora Charles. Maybe you wonder what they know that you don't and how they got so seemingly lucky. Me too. To me, they are the *blessed few.* I've always been fascinated by what these folks know, not only for my own personal reasons, but so I can be more helpful to the couples who come to me for marital therapy. There are a zillion books out there—reams of paper with advice about what to do and admonitions about what you should never do or watch out, your relationship will be doomed. I've read more than my share, along with research papers and notes from professional conferences and workshops. I've worked with hundreds of couples. And of course, I have my own experience in what seems to help and what clearly does not. Truth be told, you could probably boil all that writing down to half a dozen books, and even then there'd be a fair amount of redundancy.

That said, there are different schools of thought or—maybe more accurately—different parts of the elephant that any given theorist focuses on when looking at what it takes to create and maintain a fulfilling marriage. What I've tried to do here is look at people whose theories and methods have been resonant and useful to me, both personally and professionally, and who each have a slightly different cant on what it takes to go the distance, happily so. I've recommended the work of each of these people to clients over the years, finding that some couples might be more likely to benefit from therapist/author A and others from therapist/author B. I can usually make a reasoned guess based on their personalities and already existing strengths as a couple which approach might be most useful.

So here goes:

John Gottman:

You likely have at least a passing familiarity with John Gottman. He's probably the best-known and most widely-read researcher in the field. Gottman has spent decades in the scientific study and direct observation of the factors that improve marital stability and those that harm. This man knows from whence he speaks. In fact, in 2007, he was recognized as one of the ten most influential therapists of the past quarter century.

Maybe Gottman's most well-known concept in the field is what I referenced above—what he named the "Four Horsemen of The Apocalypse." These are the signs that portend unhealthy relationships and tend to predict divorce. The danger signs are:
- criticism;
- contempt;
- defensiveness; and
- stonewalling.

What I want to focus on here, though, is his contribution to the study of successful and satisfying marriages. *The Seven Principles for Making Marriage Work* might be his most popular book. In this book, he outlines seven principles that will reinforce the positive aspects of a relationship and help marriages endure during the rough moments.

These principles include:
- enhancing your love map (a term Gottman uses to describe the center of a person's brain where they store relevant information about their partner);
- nurturing your fondness and admiration;
- turning towards each other rather than away;
- letting your partner influence you;
- solving solvable problems;
- overcoming gridlock; and
- creating a shared meaning.

This is an even more abbreviated summary than a Reader's Digest version, but you can easily explore his work if it piques your interest.

(Here's a factoid about Gottman: while he has been married to his current wife for over three decades, he has had two previous marriages. This is not just gossip. To me it underscores just how very hard it is to make a marriage work. I mean, if *he* had to give it multiple tries, saints help the rest of us!)

Harville Hendrix:

I love the work of Harville Hendrix. His book *Getting the Love You Want* (a title that has always been a bit cringe-worthy to me) was originally published in 1988 and is still widely read. I've recommended his work to so many clients and have found it incredibly helpful personally as well. I just really jibe with everything he has to say on the subject. Hendrix developed what he termed "Imago Therapy," a style of relationship counseling that focuses on using conflict as an opportunity for growth and healing. He contends that we choose a partner that mirrors the places in us that we need to develop in ourselves; that is, our partners help us to find the places within us that need healing. It's kind of a spooky miracle, really. How the person we choose is uniquely qualified to reveal just the places in us that need to grow. How our partner will poke us right there, in that tender place, a place that may set off conflict and pain but is, in fact, our growing edge. I see this in the couples I work with about 100% of the time, plus or minus. Our unconscious is wily and smart.

Though we are rarely aware of this at the beginning of a relationship, the person we choose is ideally suited to help us work through the unfinished growth of our childhoods. We choose the perfect person to help us grow into our highest selves, a person who will (mostly) unwittingly provoke the place in us that needs healing. Here's a simple example: When Mark met Susan, he loved how assertive and strong she was because he knew he could rely on her in situations that could use a little hutzpah. And Susan really admired Mark's ability to "go with the flow" and not get spun out very often. It's the "You complete me" model. Okay, fine, but you might be able to predict what happened over time. Mark ends up feeling bullied and controlled, and Susan ends up feeling overburdened and alone. Conflict ensues and opportunity emerges. It is a safer and kind of lazier way for Mark and Susan to think about their differences as qualities they admire in each other. But if they are willing, this framing can operate as an entry into the deeper significance and *challenge* that their differences present.

A more elegant and cogent approach might be for Mark to see in Susan some under-developed parts of himself—things he personally should work on if he wants to have his fullest self, available. And ditto for Susan. As long as personality traits are divided up, there is a risk of polarizing around these traits—in this example, with Mark becoming more and more passive and Susan more aggressive, while all the while the under-developed parts of each of them slide into eventual atrophy.

I see this as the good news and the bad news all rolled into one. The good news is this: if you are ready and willing to take up the gauntlet, and by that, I mean shift the focus from what your partner is doing wrong and what s/he needs to change, and instead turn the spotlight on to yourself, the result can be amazing growth for both you and your relationship. It's like it says in the King James Bible: "And why beholdest thou the mote that is in thy brother's eye, but considerest not the beam that is in thine own eye?" Yeah, that beam. It's often hidden from us while we're busy enumerating all the helpful feedback we have for our partners about how they should change. I'll often tell couples I work with that I am sure they each have a great deal of wisdom about what their partner needs to do and how they need to change, but that it is mostly 0% useful. It's working on our own damn selves that has the highest odds of success. And if each member of a couple does that—if they individually focus on their own unfinished business—the growth both for each person and for the relationship can be an awesome thing to behold. Marriage as a people-growing machine.

The bad news part is this: If neither person in a couple is willing to turn the focus on to the unfinished parts of themselves or if only one person is, the chances of the couple developing in an elegant, truly satisfying way are slim. I get it. It's hard to grow. We resist. We don't like to change. Change can feel too difficult, too scary, and it can be so much easier to blame your partner. The pull of the status quo is so strong. The headwinds are mighty, and the impulse to settle back into the well-worn groove of the way things have always been is hard to fight against; like the snap-back of a rubber band. I wish this weren't the case, but a larger percentage of the couples I've worked with seem to find it easier, less scary, less risky and less demanding to stick with what they know.

Here's a sobering exercise: Ask yourself what it is that drives you crazy about your partner. You know, that thing s/he does that has you growling and ready to punch a wall. And then take the next step of wondering if maybe, just maybe, this reflects an underdeveloped part of you, yourself, or some trait you really need to work on. Chances are your partner is mirroring the things in you that you've been resistant to changing or maybe have been unaware of all together; the parts of yourself that you've been able to ignore or pawn off to the person you live with. Your old brain had your partner confused with your parents and believed that it had finally found the ideal candidate to make up for the psychological and emotional damage you experienced in childhood. Sit with that one.

Gary Chapman:

Gary Chapman is arguably the country's most successful marriage therapist. His book, *The 5 Love Languages*, has been on the *New York Times* best-seller list for years and continues to be very popular, to the point where it's not uncommon to hear someone at a dinner party announce, "My love language is...."

According to Chapman, these five languages are:
- words of affirmation (compliments);
- quality time;
- receiving gifts;
- acts of service; and
- physical touch.

I can totally get behind the idea of love languages though I tend to think of it a bit differently. The way I talk to my clients is by focusing on their willingness to be a *translator*. So, when Nancy tells Todd that she doesn't feel like he cares about her and he says, "What do you mean? I just took the garbage out!" I would encourage some translation. I might not use the framing of "love languages," but I could encourage Nancy to *take in* the idea that when Todd takes out the garbage, he does it because he cares about her. Translation: *I take out garbage=I care about you.* And I would also encourage Nancy to be clear and direct with Todd about what would make her feel cared about so he can extend himself in ways that may not have occurred to him. To do some translation. Chapman asserts that your partner will not feel your love if you do not speak their primary love language, even if you are fluent in the other four. It's a matter of speaking, behaving and extending yourself in ways that your partner can really *hear* you. You will each end up feeling so much more satisfied. Chapman then goes on to posit that there are five behaviors that are essential to a healthy, happy, long-term marriage:

- Love and affirmation;
- Learning how to deal with your failures through forgiveness and apology;
- Learning how to handle anger;
- Learning how to listen; and
- Accept and laugh about the minor irritations.

Esther Perel:

In 2006, Esther Perel published *Mating in Captivity*. In 2016, she was added to Oprah Winfrey's SuperSoul 100 list of visionaries and influential leaders and quickly became, if not a household name, a kind of therapist du jour. Perel's primary focus is on the tension between the erotic and the domestic. As she has said, "Never before have our expectations of marriage taken on such epic proportions. We still want everything the traditional family was meant to provide—security, children, property, and respectability—but now we also want our partner to love us, to desire us, to be interested in us. We should be best friends, trusted confidants, and passionate lovers to boot."

One of Perel's unique contributions is her focus on the challenge of reconciling security and adventure; love and desire; and connection and separateness. Our nearly universal quest for secure love can be in direct contradiction to any pursuit of passion, a state that's fueled by novelty. Perel contends that these are paradoxes, not to be solved but to be managed.

Perel's work has been recognized for its new take on intimacy. Her therapy focuses on fixing the sex first, with the contention that if you fix the sex, the relationship will follow in large part; this is about bringing more energy into a system that may have dulled through the comfort of familiarity. What we are aiming for, she asserts, is flexibility and adaptability, so that two people can engage in multiple different configurations with each other. In what some might find controversial, she contends that sexual excitement doesn't necessarily play by societal rules. It can thrive on power and is often *not* politically correct.

(Sidebar: An interesting counterpoint/companion to Perel is the approach of David Schnarch. In his books *Constructing the Sexual Crucible* and *Passionate Marriage*, Schnarch uses the lens of a couple's sex life as a metaphor for their whole relationship. Working with couples on the minute details of their sexual interaction, he focuses on each person's degree of individual differentiation and their ability to tolerate anxiety which, he contends, is the key to intimacy. So it's not exactly like Perel's contention that fixing a couple's sex life results in fixing the relationship. More, Schnarch uses an examination of a couple's sex life as a window into the broader dynamics of the relationship.)

But back to Perel. Here are some of her ideas about what it takes to sustain a healthy and happy relationship:

- Apologize first, no matter whose fault it is. To Perel, "Whoever apologizes first is always the stronger one." Apologize and take responsibility.

- Don't compare your relationship with anyone else's. (In my work, I have thousands of examples that prove you can never really know what goes on inside anyone else's house or, indeed, in anyone else's head. Afterall, we are half-opaque to ourselves to begin with.)

- Shake things up, especially in your sex life. "Love enjoys knowing everything about you; desire needs mystery." Do something new, especially if it feels a little scary. "Too often, as couples settle into the comforts of love, they cease to fan the flames of desire. They forget that fire needs air."

- Try not to feel entitled. You have the right to expect certain things—love, security, communication—but your mate does not always *owe* you. Almost all the time, a sense of entitlement comes from insecurity. Instead of a wedding vow that implies, "I will wipe every tear that streams down your face before you even notice it's going down," Perel suggests a more realistic vow would be, "I will fuck up on a regular basis, and on occasion, I'll admit it."
- Hold ambivalence. Can we accept that we can love a person without loving every single part of them? "It's an active engagement with all kinds of feelings—positive ones, primitive ones and loathsome ones."
- Love is a verb. And it's often quite surprising how it can ebb and flow. "It's like the moon; we think it has disappeared, and suddenly it shows up again." We want togetherness, and we want separateness. Coming up with a new rhythm of how to create both is a fundamental task.
- Love evolves. Renegotiate your relationship as it changes. "We will have many relationships over the course of our lives. Some of us will have them with the same person."
- Be a direct communicator and check in with each other often.
- Don't rely on your partner for everything. "Today, we turn to one person to provide what an entire village once did." Maintain a separate identity and allow yourself to feel the *otherness* of your partner.

It wasn't easy to decide on which of the zillion theorists and therapists to focus here. So many good ideas. Maybe I left out your favorite. And because it was so hard, I feel compelled to simply list more for you to explore:

- Susan Johnson's Emotionally Focused Couple Therapy (EFT): *Hold Me Tight*.

- Terrence Real's Relational Life Therapy (RLT): *The New Rules of Marriage.*
- Judith Wallerstein: *The Good Marriage.*
- And so many more.

I imagine I'm like most garden variety therapists out there who have decades of work and study under their belts. It's a little from column A, a skosh from column B, and a nod to column C. There are purists, for sure. But IMO, unless you're the actual one who created the approach, it's near impossible to stick strictly by the book. Our histories, personalities, biases and experience will transform any theory we ascribed to into an amalgam of theory + you. Personally, I've had intensive training in Person-Centered Therapy, Rational Emotive Therapy and Gestalt Therapy, as well as coursework, workshops, independent study and seminars in Cognitive-Behavioral Therapy, Psychodynamic Therapy, Jungian Therapy, and more. I'm so glad I've thrown a wide net. I feel more nimble and more able to tailor an approach that best fits the person sitting across from me.

A couple of things happened for me as I was doing a deep dive into the work of Gottman, Hendrix, Chapman and Perel. For sure, their concepts find their way into my work almost every day, and I frequently recommend their books to my clients. At the same time, this research has helped me clarify some constant and relatively simple (!) concepts that I could probably put under the heading of *My Own Personal Theory of Marital Therapy.* Things like:
- Be kind.
- Be willing and motivated to look at your own shit.
- Get as clear as you can about what the *non-negotiables* are for you in a relationship, and do your best to make peace with the rest of the inevitable pesky differences and annoyances, because guarantee, there will be.

- Communicate directly, even/especially when/if it's scary.
- Keep making deposits in your relationship bank account because you'll need a healthy balance to draw on in difficult times. If I ran the zoo, couples would laugh and dance and sing and play on a daily basis—but that's just me.
- Be *yourself*. It's a near guarantee that *not* being yourself is a recipe for dis-ease. Also, the extent to which you are *not* being yourself, you are bound to feel alone, married or not.

The other thing that happened for me when I was researching the leading thinkers in the field was, gulp, scoring myself as I went down their lists of the elements needed to create and maintain a happy, healthy marriage. My average score would probably hover between a D and a generous C+. I'm guessing that most people would have the same impulse to measure themselves against these concepts, and most likely, fall short. Aspirational, that's the best way to think about it. Realistically unattainable, but stars to shoot for. If we can plant ourselves in a trajectory that is headed for these ideals, I imagine that's the best we can hope for because, you know, human.

I've had fun seeing what some high-profile people—not just experts in the field—have said about marriage and thought I'd share some of my favorites. You might think these quotes lean in the direction of gloomy, but to me, they are more like inoculations of realism:

- "Love doesn't just sit there, like a stone, it has to be made like bread; remade all the time, made new."—Ursula K. LeGuin.
- "The most happy marriage I can imagine to myself would be the union of a deaf man to a blind woman."—Samuel Taylor Coleridge.
- "Happiness in marriage is entirely a matter of chance."—Jane Austen.
- "Keep your eyes wide open before marriage, half shut

afterwards."—Benjamin Franklin.
- "Through love scraps of copper are turned to gold."—Rumi
- "Marriage lets you annoy one person for the rest of your life."—Unknown
- "Love is a state of temporary psychosis."—Sigmund Freud
- "The mystery of love is greater than the mystery of death."-Oscar Wilde
- "Let there be spaces in your togetherness, and let the winds of the heavens dance between you. Love one another but make not a bond of love: Let it be rather a moving sea between the shores of your souls."—Kahlil Gibran.
- "We all want to be seen and loved for exactly who we are, despite our faults and failures and fuck-ups. But if it truly is unconditional love you are after, your best bet is to get a dog."—Me.

I'll close with this anecdote from a man who, when asked about the secret to his happy marriage of over six decades, said:

"Every morning I look at myself in the mirror and say, 'You're not so great either.'"

"And hand in hand, on the edge of the sand,
They danced by the light of the moon."

Edward Lear

CASE NOTES

- Christina, 42
- Andrew, 42
- Married 21 yrs
- 4 children, 8, 11, 16 and 18

PRESENTING ISSUES

Feeling distant from each other; not close as usual; short-tempered; ↑ bickering

RELEVANT HISTORY

Christina: only child; parents div when she was ~ 8 y/o; Mo bi-polar; fa "powerful & charismatic" but "unreliable"

"Perfect student" never any trouble; excelled at all she did

Andrew: youngest of 3 boys, all 2 yrs apart; "traditional fam";

- Mo nurse, fa doc; fa died in MVA when A soph in HS. Spent most of time w/ bros, not many friends til met C in HS and then they were "inseparable"

- Started dating jr yr of HS; 1st rela for both
Went to colleges near each other and after grad went to same law school; got married in law school

- A counsel for large firm; C started small firm w/ friends
Demanding but meaningful work
Both ↑ involved w/ kids, i.e., sports, camps, ex-curric stuff
Tight circle of friends, i.e., trips, parties, holidays

CLINICAL IMPRESSION:

- Sat close to each other on couch, held hands for most of session
Both tearful re not feeling close and connected
No blame or evident anger, both seemed ↑ sad

I really like these two. From the first meeting, I felt such a fondness for Christina and Andrew. But I want to clarify. 'Like' is not actually the correct word. That implies a kind of hierarchy in my feelings toward my clients. Of course, I have more simpatico with some people than with others. How could that *not* be the case? With some, I have a feeling that if we'd met in other circumstances, we might be friends. Maybe it's a similar sense of humor, world view, background, or taste in clothes. Some people just feel more like my people. But there is an amazing and wonderful thing about my work. Almost all people who come to therapy, come because they are in distress, and almost without exception, we talk intimately about their pain in ways they may not have shared with anyone else. What an awesome privilege to partner with these courageous souls! As William Butler Yeats said, "It takes more courage to examine the dark corners of your own soul than it does for a soldier to fight on a battlefield."

When a client can feel safe with me to reveal their humanity with such courage, all artifice is stripped and the ways we might be the same or different melt away in irrelevancy. So, despite meeting with people who may not have my sense of humor, who may have beliefs and opinions that are quite divergent from mine, or who do not see the world as I do, or who wear pink clothes with flowers while I wear only black, I develop such admiration for them. And time after time after time, I see that under the skin and close to the bone, despite our outer selves, we are more alike than different. The late Vietnamese monk Thich Nhat Hanh reminds us that we are individual waves in one sea all leaves of one tree. And what I see every day, with every client, is that all of us—all the leaves and all the waves—are doing what I believe we are all doing: flailing around in this muck, doing the best we can. The struggle is real, and I love them.

So yes, I do like Christina and Andrew. I love them. But let me be more specific about the feelings I had when I met with them. They were struggling, for sure. And there was pain in the room. They were feeling distant from each other. They were more quarrelsome than usual, more easily annoyed. They told me this as they sat close to each other on the couch, holding hands throughout.

I said, "Tell me what's going on."

That's pretty much all I had to say. They started in on a conversation between the two of them, me an almost invisible observer.

Christina said: "I don't know why I'm so crabby. You're not really doing anything wrong."

And Andrew said: "I'm the one who's crabby. I know I can be a dick sometimes."

And Christina said: "Come on. When have you ever been a dick? You're never a dick."

And Andrew said: "And by the way, I don't think you're crabby. I mean, with all the shit on your plate!"

They went back and forth like this for several rounds, each taking ownership of the "issues," each defending the other, which was refreshing, for sure. So many couples who seek therapy spend the session hurling insults and blame as they sit at a chilly distance from each other. With these two, the temperature in the room was warm, the mood friendly, and the discussion collaborative. Yes, refreshing, but I began to wonder if maybe they were afraid of being angry at each other. Or maybe they were out of touch with their own boundaries and needs. I wondered if they had become a kind of undifferentiated unit. David Schnarch, a renowned expert (some say renegade) in the field of marital therapy, asserted that a marriage cannot succeed unless each person claims a sense of *self in the presence of the other*. He wrote about the tension between attachment and autonomy and believed that our preoccupation with attachment, with its ideal of feeling and acting as one, keeps partners infantile and overly emotionally dependent—enmeshed in the language of psychology; fused is the way Schnarch put it. He contended that marital attachment doesn't leave enough space for partners to speak their own minds, think their own thoughts, or attain their individual ambitions and dreams.

Here's another decision therapists need to make: when to risk breaking a good mood, when to explore difficult issues when things seem to be going well, in other words, when to be a buzzkill. Personally, I believe that it is *therapeutic* to talk about exactly *how* things are going well (i.e., to explore more deeply rather than just say, "Cool. That's great. I'm happy you're doing well.") After all, it's not like the good stuff just rained down from the sky. We actually have to *do* or *think* or *feel* in order to create these positive changes. I've found it to be reinforcing to ask a client, "So how did you make this happen for yourself? Exactly how are you each making things better?" I get answers like, "I was more patient," or "I decided I wouldn't let X bother me today," or "I've been focusing on gratitude," or a zillion other ways that we have the power to affect our mood and circumstance.

At the same time, for a therapist to avoid raising issues that may rock the boat or spoil the mood or alienate the client is, I believe, a fairly wimpy stance to take and—to risk sounding overly dramatic—a kind of dereliction of duty. The goal of therapy—which is sometimes an uncomfortable and unwelcome reality for people new to the process—is *not* to leave each session feeling good. Rather, the over-arching goal is to facilitate growth, and often that doesn't feel very good in the process.

Back to Christina and Andrew. To test the water and explore whether there might be some unhealthy enmeshment, I said:

"Christina, are there ways in which you think Andrew might be behaving in a dick-ish way?"

And:

"Andrew, I'm wondering if Christina actually has seemed crabbier than usual."

They looked at each other before either answered. I see this happen a lot when working with couples, and it almost always feels kind of—I'm going to use a very over-used word here—co-dependent to me. When I ask one person a question, before answering, they look at their partner, and the thought bubble I see over their head is, *Is it okay if I answer? I'm worried you'll be upset or angry if I say what I'm thinking. I'm afraid you won't see it the way I do. I don't want to hurt your feelings.* So, by co-dependent, I mean how we hold ourselves back from saying or doing something for fear of how the other will respond. With this couple, I wondered if Christina might be willing to describe some of Andrew's behaviors as dick-ish if it were just she and I talking, but feel reluctant to say so in his presence, probably because she would not want to risk hurting his feelings. And same-same for Andrew.

I'm glad I tested the enmeshment theory out and was relieved when I heard:

Christina (looking at Andrew): "Okay, yes. I get it, with all the stress, but it's true. I really don't like how impatient you've been, but you've been kind of an asshole, taking it out on the kids and me. You've got to find a better way, babe."

Andrew (looking at Christina): "Ouch, give me a sec cuz I'm about to get defensive (takes a few breaths). I don't want to be that guy—but it seems like you are so overloaded, and a lot of the time you just don't seem very happy. Like you don't have time for me. And like I can't do anything right."

We explored further, and I shelved my concerns about

enmeshment, at least for the time being. And in terms of what brought them to therapy, it really didn't take a trained professional to suss out what led to the distance they were experiencing. These were two people in demanding professions. They were highly committed to quality family time and had very active children who were in multiple extracurriculars and played multiple sports. They had a large and vibrant circle of friends, and they made sure to nurture those relationships. On top of all that, Christina's mother was Bipolar, on and off her medication. It's kind of amazing they recognized each other at the breakfast table! With all of the demands on their time and attention, their couple-hood had slipped quietly and progressively down the priority list. That's where the focus of our work was: on ways to honor and nurture and attend to their partnership.

Christina and Andrew displayed a rather extraordinary degree of attributes that I don't often witness in the couples I see—things like openness, willingness to take responsibility, non-defensiveness, and a readiness to accept influence by the other. I see so much angst in relationships—including the ones I've been in myself. So much fear and unmet (and usually unrealistic) expectations. Our primary relationships are where we tend to have the most at stake, and because of that, they are where we regress the most, where our primitive selves somehow feel safer to come out and play. I see this as the good news and the bad news all rolled into one. Maybe you think you somehow have progressed beyond having any of these primitive, regressive feelings. If so, I have a crown and scepter for you. For the rest of us mortals, we have the chance to think of these limbic brain responses as our growing edge, the place to focus if we are motivated to continue on a path of psychological/emotional/spiritual growth. In this way, marriage is like a people-growing machine. It holds a mirror up to us and lets us see parts of ourselves that do not tend to make an appearance in other venues. *That! Right there. That place that keeps getting poked at. That's some unfinished business. That's what I need to work on!*

I don't know what this couple's relationship was like in their earlier years. When I met them, they'd already been married for twenty-one years. And I don't know their history of individual work. Also—bear with me here—maybe they are somewhere along a particular karmic path. If that sounds whacky to you, I get it. For me, the older I get, the more seems possible. But when I met with Christina and Andrew, I felt hopeful and sanguine. I don't mean to imply that it is uncommon for me to feel optimistic in my work. It can be thrilling to witness one small chip fall away in what is almost always a rock-chipping process. Change can happen imperceptibly unless you are paying close attention…and that's definitely part of my job, paying close attention. So, when another client, who had been practically phobic about conflict of any kind, tells me that her friend suggested they go out for sushi, and she replied that she'd rather have Thai, I wanted to break out the party hats. She didn't think it was such a big deal, but that's mostly what this work is: rock-chipping. *I'd rather have Thai, thank you very much.* That's a win in my book.

So yes, there are many times in my work when I feel uplifted and hopeful and buoyed by the power of the process. But one thing I do have anecdotal evidence of: most couples who come to therapy come as a kind of last resort. It's true that pain and suffering are almost always the impetus for seeking therapy in general, but in my experience and anecdotally, individuals do not seem to wait till they are one breath from the end. With couples, however, it's almost always a case of *in extremis*, but not so with this Andrew and Christina.

Right now I'm worried I may be mis-understood. When I read

back what I just wrote, I wonder if you may think I'm suggesting, implying, or even forewarning in some kind of way: *You, you guys who are thinking of coming to me for couple's work: I expect you to be highly functioning, with minimal and easy-to-work-with issues. If that's not the case, I may judge you. I may not like you, and I may not even want to work with you at all.*

Nope. Not at all. No. As I said before, it is my firmly, deeply, wholeheartedly held belief that we are *all*, every one of us, flailing around in this life, trying our best, sometimes inching forward, sometimes not. Wherever we are on any given day or month or year, or yes, *even* on some kind of karmic path, is where we are. I hold profound respect and love for *all* the people who choose to engage in the brave pursuit of introspection, wherever they may be on their journey.

So, let me try to explain further what I mean about the feelings I had when working with Christina and Andrew. First of all, I felt pretty confident that I could help them. Some people's circumstances are knottier than others. And sometimes, the complexities and the gravity of the issues make me unsure about how our work will unfold, and whether or not I will be able to help. I can get seduced by the (irrational) belief that if a marriage fails after working with me, it is my fault; if I can't improve their dynamics, then I have failed. There's a line here, a distinction between what *is* my job and what is a remnant of my co-dependent and ego-based impulse to regularly assume responsibility for others' feelings and behavior. It *is* my job to facilitate the process, to observe and communicate the dynamics as I see them, and to use the tools I have developed to help them improve the ways they relate to each other. It is *not* my job (I remind myself) to take ownership of any particular outcome. In this particular case, I'm not sure that line even existed for me to ponder. My function with Christina and

Andrew, as I came to see it, was to provide a stress-free, quiet, and safe place for them to talk to each other and to serve as a witness. I felt relieved of any residue of anxiety about my ability to help.

Also, there was a quality to their relationship that shone through and permeated the room, like the molecules took on a different quality. They had such obvious high regard for each other, so much fondness. There was a sense of ease and softness. Missing was what so many of us (read: me) can exhibit when our relationship is struggling: prickliness, peevishness, defensiveness. With them, there was a sense of elasticity and degrees of freedom, even when they were expressing a grievance. They seemed genuinely curious about how the other thought and felt. And it was clear that they were firmly rooted in the principle of giving each other the benefit of the doubt. These are characteristics that John Gottman has defined as crucial for a relationship's success. For sure, they had a good reason for coming in. But it felt more like getting a manicure when your cuticles are a wreck. Relationship maintenance.

One more thing about my emotional experience with this couple. Maybe you can relate to this: you know someone who has so many gifts, so many blessings, so much good fortune that there is a part of you that could easily descend into envy and even antagonism? *She's so perfect...I hate her!* But she's also someone you really like/love and who has been willing to be her flawed human self with you, so that actually there is hardly any room for even a sliver of disdain. Okay, maybe some envy still exists, but you can recognize it as your pesky ego at work. We can't ever entirely rid ourselves of that primitive part of ourselves, after all. When we are responding from our ego, we are not operating from a paradigm of abundance. We're out on the tundra trying to save ourselves from marauding wild animals. But we can increase the amount of time we spend in our *higher* selves and not let ourselves pay too much attention to our primordial impulses.

One of the unanticipated benefits of doing this work is that I have had a front-row seat and daily practice with the aphorism variously credited to Anne Lamott, the actor Rob Lowe, and twelve-step groups like Alcoholics Anonymous: "Never compare your insides to someone else's outsides." Out in the real world, my envy may have had more room to exert its presence had I encountered Christina and Andrew, say, at a dinner party. But in my office, I witness the inside of people on the daily, making it much harder to judge myself against anyone's outside. It's true that I have not had the good fortune to reach the place that this couple has on their marital journey. I wish I had. I can feel the dregs of envy, yes. But in my work with them—in this confined and time-out-of-time and yes, sacred space—the part of me that can still measure and compare and find myself wanting just didn't find much oxygen.

You might be wondering what happened with this couple. I don't know. If I were asked to make a wager on their future, I'd bet big money that they would survive. More than survive. There are plenty of couples who stay together for decades—stay out of fear or complacency or because of the undeniable pull of the status quo. That's not what I mean. Both as individuals and as a couple, I believe that Christina and Andrew have the ingredients—most specifically the openness, goodwill, and dedication to the process—to predict a strong bond throughout their lives together. That said, I've been surprised before. Surprised about relationships that end up flourishing when they seemed so flawed and surprised when I see a relationship that seemed so healthy end up falling apart. What goes on in the crucible of marriage is complex, enigmatic, and often opaque to anyone outside the system. You may think you know what's going on behind their closed door, but I encourage you to think again.

"Oh love, you break on me like light!"

Sophocles

When I turned fifty, I threw myself a party. I only invited my girlfriends. I bought a ton of good champagne, got take-out from the upscale deli and had tee-shirts made for everyone, black with white print: *girlfriends rule!* I was about two years out from my last divorce, and I was feeling good.

Sometimes it takes getting smacked upside your head to get a lick of sense. After so much failure in the marriage department, the verdict was in. No way could I chalk it up to being ill-starred or snakebit. I couldn't blame karma or mercury in retrograde, at least if I wanted to keep a straight face. I could not hide from myself one second longer. Let the idioms fly: the carrots were cooked, the jig was up, and the fat lady had left the stage. I'm done world! I am clearly no good at this marriage thing, so I. Am. Out!

Do I sound defensive? It's possible, of course, that I was fooling myself in my effort to fool the world. Or vice versa. Maybe. I do remember a shift, though. As far back as I could remember, I was a boy-crazy female. My self-concept and my sense of worth were always so intimately tied to whether or not I had a boy/man in my life. Oh, I did a mighty imitation of a competent, independent female. And if I'm being objective, I was/am a competent female. I'm smart enough, educated enough, savvy enough, worldly enough—all things I knew even then.

But independent? Not existentially needy of a man? Hard to admit, but no. This sort of bifurcated view of myself has been confusing for me as long as I can remember, though if I put on my psychologist hat and heard this story from a client, I would say, "I hear so much impatience with yourself. So much criticism. Things are always more complicated than that. There can be so many reasons why, despite being competent and capable, you have felt needy and dependent."

But back to the shift. There I was at fifty, and like I said, about two years from my last divorce. It had been the most painful, this last one. For starters, come on! How could this be happening again? How could I show my face out there in the world? How could I accommodate the shame? And the particulars were an ego hit that was new to me. An affair, a pregnancy! I remember this question, this endless feedback loop with me constantly like a leitmotif: "What am I going to do? What am I going to do?" From this distance, that seems like quite an odd question. Exactly what did I mean, "What am I going to do?" Did I imagine there was some thing I was *supposed* to do? Right then? The next day? Something that I *shouldn't* do? Something I could do that would change the reality? Some magic thing that would make it all go away? I felt that question with such urgency, "What am I going to do?"

(Sidebar: I have come to hear questions like this—*What am I going to do? Why is this happening? How could you do this to me?*—not really as questions, but as statements. Yes, they have a question word at the beginning, and a question mark slapped at the end, but really I think they are passionate existential outcries. My "question"—*What am I going to do?*—was a cri de coeur: *I hate that this is happening, and I am so very scared.*)

I don't think eureka moments happen very often in life, but I woke up one day with this neon-lit insight: *Here's what you're going to do. You're going to live your life, woman!* Maybe that sounds like a big, giant *DUH,* but I can only say that for me it was a revelation.

I have a life. A life of my own. And I am going to live this life, this life that is mine. The eureka-ness of it was this: live or die, that's my choice. I don't mean die as in suicide. I mean die as in a spiritual, emotional, psychological, soul-sucking death. True, black is my color, but the thought of moving through whatever was left of my life—what might have been a full second half—as a phantasma of sorts, was one of the choices before me. Like Albert Camus said—in a quote that to me sounds more like Woody Allen—"Should I kill myself, or have a cup of coffee?" I was standing at the crossroads of a binary choice, and that was the insight, the insight that led to the shift.

(One more sidebar: In my work, I've been fascinated by the concept of *readiness*. What does it take for someone to be ready to finally take in some feedback, to change? I've had the experience with clients where I might have given the same feedback a zillion times, and then, for no explicable reason, on the zillionth+one time, they hear it as if for the first time. The image that works best for me is a glass of water that fills one drop at a time until, finally, one drop spills over. The totality of our history fills that glass over time, and the final drop can be anything, even the smallest thing: a word, an expression, a dream. Or the simple passage of time. Readiness.)

By the time I threw that party, I'd been living this insight for a couple of years. I had purchased a townhouse, plopping down my own damn money and signing the endless stack of papers that needed only my signature and my initials—mine alone. I moved to a neighborhood where I could walk almost everywhere, something I'd wanted forever. I got a cat. I entertained the friends I loved. I went where I wanted to go and didn't go where I didn't want to go. The way I came to think about it was this: everywhere I went, I took my *whole* self with me. I felt this sense of completeness. For better or worse, there was no person waiting at home for me. No check-in required, no call if I chose to stay late. No piece of me and no bit of attention waiting home while I was out. The one and only criterion was what *I* wanted. Just me. It wasn't a good or bad, right or wrong, better or worse thing. It was me leaning in to the particular joys that living a single life can bring. It was the apples side of the idiom. It was God's gift to me: a truckload of Thin Mints, Samoas and Tagalongs.

And then.

I met Donna waiting for the bus on the first day of kindergarten. She would be my best friend all through school. It wasn't just that we lived across the street from each other or that we were the same age, or that we were in the same classroom. It had to do with meaning. Each of us was in a very challenging home environment—different from each other, but neither home was what I would call a safe and secure place. The dysfunction of our parents created a void that we filled for each other. We trusted each other. We needed each other. We grew each other up. Yes, our lives diverged after we left for college, and our contact was sporadic over the years, but she is embedded deep in my psyche in a way that feels biologic and most definitely permanent.

So, when she called me—not too long after that fiftieth birthday party—and told me about this guy, this co-worker of hers, this man she thought was amazing, this divorced and available man, this man who would be traveling to Oregon where I was living even though he lived in New York—when she called me and said *I really think you should meet him, he's such a great guy*—if it had been someone else, anyone else, I'm not sure what I would have said. But it was Donna.

I'm not trying to imply that this is a better or healthier or more-evolved or preferable template for relationships, not at all. But my experience in meeting W was different from any other similar experience that I'd had in the past. No instant attraction. No feeling of kismet. No oh-shit-I'm-in-trouble feeling. At least on my part. And if he hadn't felt some of those things toward me, who knows, the relationship might have gone nowhere, especially because we lived a country apart from each other. But he did, so he pursued.

On that first meeting, I made some excuse to duck out for a minute and call a local girlfriend. She was in on all of this and waiting to hear how it was going, so I called her and said, "Yes, he's super nice, seems like a great guy. I just met him, but somehow I feel like I can totally trust him; no, not feeling lusty feelings; yes, he's attractive, might be great to have him as a friend, who knows, yeah, I might see him again before he leaves, maybe."

Which I did.

And when I called my friend after that second meeting, I said all the same things.

And then.

A few weeks later, Donna called to say that she and W would be going to northern California on a work trip and why didn't I fly down and meet them for the weekend; no pressure, I could bunk with her, and we could just have a fun time in lovely Santa Rosa.

Which—after hemming and hawing and mostly thinking no but finally saying okay, fine, why not—I went.

This is a sad story.

W and I only had three years together. If you asked me if I believe we'd still be married today, I would say yes, empathically yes. But I also know that everyone believes their love will go the distance from the beginning vantage point when the bloom is still on the rose. But who knows what the ensuing years would have brought us. Challenges for absolutely sure! And three years is not enough time to feel confident about how each of us would have risen to whatever vagaries landed at our doorstep. And who knows how each of us may have changed and how those changes would have impacted our partnership. Not me; I sure don't know.

What I *do* know, however, is that my relationship with W was different from any I'd had before. Yeah, I know: *all* relationships are different from each other, but still. Probably the most significant factor is how *I* had changed before meeting him. It was so many things. It was the passage of time. It was the heartaches. It was the accretion of the enlightening experiences of engaging deeply with hundreds of clients. It was my regular come-to-Jesus meetings with myself. It was the mystery of readiness. All of it had tempered me. I hardly recognized that boy-crazy chick. She was the one who would see the guy way back there—the one who's a bundle of neuroses, all seductive swagger, draped in red flags—and say, *Hey you, over there, step right up. Oh, you say you're a bundle of neuroses? Addicted to something or other? Or a hot-mess project in some other way? Yes, you! Come on up!* That girl seems rather quaint in my memory. Finally and belatedly and blessedly, I had a sense of wholeness and a rock-ribbed belief in my own enough-ness.

I'll just list the characteristics of my relationship with W that bolster my belief that we had a good chance of making it last*:

—forbearance and patience;
—not taking things personally;
—being on the same side;
—respecting and celebrating our differences and individuality;
—whatever the opposite of co-dependence is;
—affectionate teasing;
—dealing with whatever crap arose whenever it did;
—good sex.

* None of these perfectly or all the time, but mostly and usually.

But still, I don't really know how things between us would have unfolded over time had he not died.

Also, this is *not* a sad story.

Do you know this Tim McGraw song?: "Someday I hope you get the chance to live like you were dying." I know what he means. I am grateful for the experience of living with death on my shoulder for almost two years. Of course, that's not entirely accurate. It was hell in so many ways, and the intensity of the experience—living in the relentless mode of flight or flight—probably ravaged my body and my psyche in any number of ways. And yet, since we knew that *future* for us was months at best, the bulk of the time we had was spent firmly in the present. Time is a weird construct, my friends, and relativity served us so well. Those seconds, minutes and hours stretched out farther than I ever knew they could. We spent months in every hour. Ram Dass could have pointed at us excitedly and said, *Yes! This is what I mean: BE HERE NOW*!

For this, I am grateful.

I will confidently say that romantic relationships are over for me—even though as I say this, I have to swat away a taunting and pesky background presence: that fickle finger of fate, that"…unseen and unforeseeable force that controls the direction of all living things." Okay, true. I am quite aware of how notoriously bad we humans are at predicting the future. But whatever is in store for me is not really the point here anyway. What makes relationships work and what causes trouble is what I'm interested in. And after all these years and all my training and all my research and all the experts I've consulted, all of my own experiences, and all the clients I've had the privilege to engage with, what emerges are persistent themes—things that predict (not perfectly, *of course*) marital satisfaction and things that portend (but don't guarantee) marital dissolution. Those theorists have a ton of wisdom.

And yet.

I don't want to sound doctrinaire. I can easily find exceptions to these concepts, and I've seen relationships that hurl a ton of defiance at all the scholarly wisdom. And praise the powers that be; I hope we never forget how much paradox and mystery and magic there is at work in the world. That said, I see so much evidence—including in my own life—that a combination of feeling personally *enough* + being willing to examine yourself with clear eyes seems to be a pretty great formula, not just for attracting a worthy partner but for whatever other path your life takes.

Afterword

I saw the dissolution of my parents' marriage and also the parents of my best friend who lived across the street. In the house next door, another friend's father committed suicide, and her mother's next marriage ended in divorce. The older couple who lived where the road took a sharp bend divorced, and so did the parents of the kid a year behind me who lived on the other side of the woods behind my house.

I could go on.

I was a kid of the fifties, glued to every episode of *I Love Lucy*, *Leave it to Beaver*, and *Father Knows Best*. Visiting those families was like going to Venus. Where I grew up, it was more like *The Ice Storm*, Rick Moody's book and subsequent movie. Morally bankrupt, that's how I think of it. In the world of the Ricardos and Cleavers and Andersons, the problems they dealt with were things like Lucy insisting on driving the new car or Ward conflicted over which son to take to the championship baseball game or Bud lying about his age to get a job as a stock clerk. Not a whiff of the dark underbelly that pervaded our New York City suburb. The TV families were so happy, so stable, and so wholesome. It wasn't just that divorce was nowhere to be seen. There was no alcohol, no key parties, and no affairs. In my world—in affluent Fairfield County, Connecticut, planet earth—all of that was de rigueur, if not in the open, at least without much effort to hide. We kids knew. In fact, my friend and I—when we were maybe eight or nine—were sent on an errand by her mother—*Hop on your bikes and see what you can find out about that other woman.* We didn't mind. In fact, we didn't give it a second thought. We also loved Nancy Drew. We jumped on our bikes and came back with a report.

That's just plain wrong. Twisted.

I see that now.

Romantic relationships, marriage, and coupledom have been fascinating to me forever. I wonder if this interest was fueled by this stark contrast: the ideal beamed into my living room on that massive mahogany console and the realities of our lived lives.

There are other reasons for this fascination. Despite the true fact that my mother was hardly the stereotypical housewife—always working, always striving, always creating—still she was most definitely what you'd call a man's woman. She hated being without a man and never let any time elapse between marriages. She was flirtatious and seductive and not a good friend to the women in her life. The unspoken message *You're No One Without a Man* drowned out the message *You are Enough.*

I was boy-crazy from adolescence.

No wonder.

No wonder, also, that my paradigm of marriage was what it was.

I've been a psychologist in private practice for over forty years, and for that long I've specialized in seeing couples. Other therapists I know prefer not to do this kind of work. They might say they don't like being in the presence of so much conflict. Or that it's depressing to witness so many relationships fall apart. Me, I love this work. I love understanding whatever dynamic is at play and how their individual issues show up, often outside their conscious awareness. It's a fascinating puzzle to me. And I have developed a kind of shield that protects me from absorbing most of the conflict, and conflict indeed there is.

But that strikes me as a glib explanation.

In my fascination, in my work to understand a couple's dynamic and learn how their individual histories show up in their relationship, I'm trying to solve my own puzzle. Is the ideal TV marriage possible? Or is what I witnessed in my own real-life growing-up experience more real? Was I doomed from the jump? I've been working to figure this out forever.

It makes so much sense that I am a psychologist. We are attracted to what we need.

If I were on a debate team, I could argue both sides. I could defend the joys and blessings that only come from an enduring and loving partnership, one that has met all the challenges that would inevitably arise, one that has grown and accommodated and met the test of maturity. Or I could switch sides and assert the undeniable fact that who we are at twenty-five is not who we are at fifty, and how could you possibly make a life-long decision given how change happens? And that the standard of a happy sixty-plus-year marriage is outdated and unrealistic. And that having serial relationships is more congruent with the construct of partnership as a source of growth and meaning. Also, being married and being single is an apples-and-oranges comparison.

Also, maybe I have some baked-in cynicism.

Even so.

After all this exploration and study and thought, where I land now is on the who-knows of it all. There are general principles about how to create an enduring partnership, of course. Like *Be Nice*. But I remember a couple I worked with many years ago. They spent every session hurling vile insults at each other way—and I mean *way* below the belt, until I had to intervene and practically tape their mouths shut because I couldn't bear it anymore. And after they left my office, I would watch from my seventh-floor window as they walked to their car, arm in arm, stopping every few feet to kiss. And what I thought was, *This is odd, they'll never last*, but they would come back periodically over the years, still together.

And another couple I know. They met in their freshman year of college, had one date and then moved in together. If I'd known them at the time, I would have thought, *This is odd, they'll never last*, but they've been married for over forty years, and from what I can tell, happily so.

Oh, Sweet Mystery of Life.

One of the things I focus on when I'm working with a couple or with an individual who is struggling in their relationship is to help them clarify what for them are the non-negotiables in a marriage. Experience has taught me that there will always be differences that are beyond aggravating, things that we will eventually have to eye-roll and shrug off, things way beyond *Why in the holy hell can you not put the goddam dish in the dishwasher when it's literally right where you are standing*. I mean big things. That said, I do believe that the exercise of discerning what is a negotiable (read: tolerable) difference, and one that is non-negotiable, is a crucial exercise for one's well-being. And one thing I learn over and over again is that what for me would be a nothing burger, might be a non-negotiable for someone else.

A perfect example: years ago, I worked with a woman who was on the brink of leaving her husband of thirty-six years. Her main beef was that he never gave her what she called "thoughtful presents," instead marking important occasions with flowers and chocolate. You might think her focus on the gift thing was actually about something else, something deeper. Me too, I assumed that myself and did my best to explore, but got exactly nowhere. I'm not sure what happened with them, but—and I will cop to some judgment here—I hope that she discovers that indeed there is some deeper meaning to her about the gift thing, and that she doesn't stick to the story that receiving certain kinds of gifts is a non-negotiable for her. But who am I to say.

This is perfect work to do with a therapist, this whole process of sifting through the inevitable points of conflict that result from our differences and determining what we can abide, albeit with teeth clenched and begrudging acceptance or what is too deeply compromising.

It's tempting to believe that there's a right way. I/we/you/they might have ideas and opinions and judgments and our own baked-in paradigms about some standard to strive for, some white whale, some Instagram vision that makes the rest of us feel forever wanting. I've spent my long career with so much access into people's inner lives, and still—and maybe *because*—I do believe that we can never really know another in their totality, so how could we possibly judge the way they might choose to pair up or not? There are so many ways to do marriage. A long marriage that has been full of conflict and disappointment might also give each person a sense of stability and safety in a way that a more stable, vibrant relationship might not. Truly an apples-and-oranges comparison. Our values are tempered by our singular experience, and while I might put a premium on emotional and psychological growth—required orientation for a psychologist, no doubt—I am reminded every day that my lens is mine, and yours might be entirely different.

Also, am I painting a grim picture? Realistic, I hope. This is about *people*, after all, and we people are messy, messy beings. We all have our pathologies and imperfections. We are each of us a pain in the ass sometimes. Or, to paraphrase Swami Prabhupada (founder of the Hare Krisha Movement), being human is an embarrassing situation. When all is said and done—and then theorized and admonished and prescribed—maybe it's just whatever gets you through the night.

Author's Notes

This is a book of personal nonfiction as close to what my flawed and spotty memory could recall. It is, primarily, a book of my own journey on the rock-ribbed path of romance.

My ex-husbands, of course, know who they are. And to my friends: you may know them too.. For those of you who have no personal knowledge of me, I hope and trust that what I've written about them does not betray their identities. They sure didn't ask for this. These are not full histories, of course. Much was very good. And if one of them happens by some extremely weird and unlikely circumstance to pick up this book, I'd like to say this: It has been my deeply held intention to take an as objective look as possible at our relationships. Each time I sat down to write the sections about our marriages—the hardest ones to write, you won't be surprised to hear—I put on a metaphorical vest and Stetson, sat in front of a shiny black Remington and did my most earnest imitation of a dispassionate reporter who had no ax to grind, *nothing but the facts*. These were the sections that I pored over—relentlessly, repeatedly, mercilessly—demanding of myself, *Girl, are you taking at least your fair share?*

That said, where my feet are planted is the vantage point that I have and you guys would, I am quite sure, have a different story to tell.

All the clients I have written about are composites. I have removed any details that could in any way identify the brave souls I've had the privilege to work with. If you see any resemblance to yourself or anyone you know, I promise you are mistaken. Coincidence.

My intention here was to take a fearless look at what worked and didn't work in my own marriages and use that exploration to uncover whatever general principles were at work and how they manifested in couples I have seen in my practice. What I continually reminded myself: relationships are complicated animals; it's never just one thing, for good or for bad. I did not intend for this to be an extensive, inclusive examination of all the many factors that influence the success or undoing of marital relationships. There are bookstore shelves bulging with advice about what to do, what never to do, what's bad, what's good, and watch out for this or that. Instead, I've focused on specific concepts/challenges/sticky points that seem to come up with enough frequency that you might be able to relate and finally explore what seems to help. Something, I hope, might have whet your appetite.